WORKING WISDOM

LISTS FOR IMPROVING YOUR BUSINESS!

Thomas J. Leonard

AUSTIN

Working Wisdom
The Top 10 Lists for Improving Your Business!

Copyright © 1997 by Sandy Vilas and Thomas J. Leonard

Printed in Canada

Write or call Bard Press,
1515 Capital of Texas Highway, S., Suite 205,
Austin, Texas 78746, phone (512) 329-8373, fax (512) 329-6051.

ISBN: 1-885167-26-1

Library of Congress Cataloging-in-Publication Data

Leonard, Thomas J., 1995–
    Working wisdom : top 10 lists for improving your business / Thomas
J. Leonard.
        p.   cm.
    ISBN 1-885167-26-1
    1. Industrial management—Miscellanea.   2. Business—Miscellanea.
3. Vocational guidance—Miscellanea.   I. Title.
HD38.L3943   1997   97-28851
658—dc21   CIP

To order additional copies, contact your local bookstore
or call (800) 945-3132 or fax (512) 288-5055.

The author may be contacted at the following address:
        Coach University
        2484 Bering Drive
        Houston, Texas 77057

Visit our Web site at www.bardpress.com.

A BARD PRESS BOOK

Copyeditor: Steve Welch
Proofreaders: Deborah Costenbader, Doreen Piano
Cover Design: Hugh Pirnie
Text Design/Production: Suzanne Pustejovsky
Text Composition: Round Rock Graphics

First Printing, September 1997

WORKING WISDOM

Thomas Leonard did not want to write an introduction to this book, so he gave me the task. At first, I groaned; then I saw it as an opportunity to let others know what a remarkable man he is—a man with an amazing gift of genius and vision, as you will see when you read this book. I also accepted the mission because he is a friend—a loyal, supportive, generous friend.

I first met Thomas Leonard in 1989 in San Francisco. I was starting a training business, and in a three-weekend session, he began teaching me the art and science of being a personal and business coach. Although I used my new skills sparingly over the next five years, this was the beginning of a wonderful friendship.

That relationship has since taken many exciting turns. Thomas began personally coaching me in 1992. We shared a Houston office in 1993 while he was founding Coach University. All along, he kept exhorting me to start a coaching practice of my own—which I did, hesitantly, in 1994.

Over the next two years, I coached 250 clients, helping them achieve the things that mattered most to them. Almost immediately, I quadrupled my income. More important, I found the joy, satisfaction, and peace that had long eluded me. I loved every minute of it.

In July 1996, Thomas offered me the opportunity to buy Coach University. I jumped at it. At that time, Coach University had 500 students enrolled in the two-year teleclass program—and one employee, recently hired. Today, a staff of ten serves 1,400 students from more than thirty countries.

Thomas began writing top-ten lists a few years ago. They were so well received that he turned out more than 800 of them, covering mostly business, personal, and coaching issues. Now they are on the World Wide Web (www.coachu.com), and more than 5,000 people get daily top-ten lists free via e-mail subscriptions.

This book is a distillation of the wisdom of Thomas's lists. Designed for people who have little time to wade through today's ceaseless flow of information, *Working Wisdom* offers quick nuggets of practical and easy-to-use ideas for improving business effectiveness.

I am very grateful to have Thomas as a friend, partner, and coach. He has given the world the gift of coaches, the ripple effect of which will be felt for decades. That legacy alone would be enough for most people—but not Thomas. He sits in front of his Mac and pours out one brilliant piece after another, all of which contribute greatly to the well-being of people worldwide. Thank you, Thomas, for the many gifts you give so freely to others.

Sandy Vilas

President, Coach University
July 1997

CONTENTS IN BRIEF

TABLE OF CONTENTS

PART 1

SALES & MARKETING

PART 2

ENTREPRENEURSHIP

P A R T   3

CUSTOMER SERVICE

P A R T   4

ELECTRONIC OFFICE

P A R T   5

POSITIVE RESULTS

P A R T   6

INSPIRED MANAGEMENT

P A R T 7
BUSINESS WISDOM

1

SALES & MARKETING

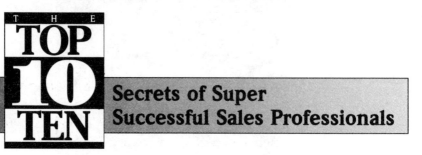

The top 5 percent of all sales professionals seem to have most of the following qualities, traits, styles, and attitudes. I've included the corresponding traditional selling skill in parentheses. Obviously, these top 10 secrets go the next step beyond the traditional way of describing them.

1. They have an obvious and compelling passion for people, not just for the product or service.

(Old: They really believe in the product or service.)

Super Sales Professionals care so much for people and helping them to solve their problems that the buyer feels this. It's not an act; it's a calling.

2. They have an ability to help the prospective customer *feel* enthusiastic.

(Old: They find pain.)

The Super Sales Professional doesn't just look for the hot buttons as a way of getting the person to buy. Instead, they help to create a possibility that excites the buyer.

3. **They have a willingness to sell to the buyer's buying strategy instead of using a collection of selling techniques and hoping for a connection.**

(Old: They use a technique that works for the customer.)

This requires a certain humility because the Super Sales Professional makes the buyer more important than the Super Sales Professional's collection of selling skills. Buyers have their preferred ways to purchase; get to know these in general and quickly discover the preferred way that your potential customer buys.

4. **They have an ability to discern who is going to be a buyer and who is not.**

(Old: They have an ability to qualify prospects quickly.)

Super Sales Professionals have a sixth sense that helps them to distinguish between tire kickers and real buyers. This sixth sense can be developed, and it saves lots of time and frustration when mastered.

5. **They have an ability to match the *exact* features of the product with the client's needs.**

(Old: Sell the sizzle, not just the steak.)

No buyer cares about all of the features and benefits; they usually only care about one or two of them. Your mission: Sense, feel, or discover (by asking questions and assessing the situation) the key benefits that turn this discussion into a sale quickly.

6. They don't seem desperate to make the sale.

(Old: Don't appear too hungry.)

Hungry salespeople scare away the meal.

7. They discern the appropriate next step for the buyers and help them see how the seller's product or service is the obvious choice.

(Old: Sell to the need.)

This requires some thinking and feeling. When you can size up your buyers and look ahead with them, you can help them see how your product or service can assist them in their progress.

8. They have plenty of evidence of how *really* valuable the product or service is and can communicate it to customers with confidence.

(Old: Know your product or service well.)

When you've seen enough customers do extremely well with your product or service, you won't be hesitant to share how well it works. Facts inspire confidence. Get to know the real facts about how effectively your product or service performs and delights customers, and you'll be a fearless sales professional.

9. They bring benefits to everyone they touch, buyer or not.

(Old: Be a resource to potential customers.)

Either you try to help everyone or you don't.

10. They are human, light, and "real" with everyone.

(Old: Create rapport.)

Drop the pretense, the false sincerity, the I'm-your-new-best friend, the I'm-here-to-serve-you-at-least-as-long-as-I-think-there's-a-chance-that-you'll-buy-something-from-me.

Things to Say or Do When a Prospective Customer Says No

1. Clarify the no.

"Is that no for now, no forever, or no, I don't like you?"

2. Identify the no.

"Most people say no to this product at first. Would you tell me which part you are saying no to?"

3. Accept the no.

"I understand completely. It's worth thinking about first."

4. Keep talking and listening.

"I accept your no, Bob. But can we discuss it?"

5. Ask a thinking question.

"Would you tell me where you want to be financially in ten years, Bob?"

6. Ask an empathy question.

"Is it the price, Bob?"

7. Ask a trick question.

"If I can completely resolve your concerns about this product, would you be inclined to buy?"

8. Ask for permission to ask again.

"OK, Bob, I hear you. Will you give me the option of letting you know of any news regarding this product over the course of the next 12 months?"

9. Get some other energy in there.

"Bob, would you find it helpful if I asked a happy customer of mine to call you this week to share his experience of this product? He won't sell you, but you can ask him any questions."

10. Get permission to keep in touch.

"May I send you my quarterly newsletter for a year?"

Techniques to Double-Close the Sale

Getting a yes from a prospective customer or client is just the first step in benefiting from the sale. You need to ensure that the customer really does buy and that their purchase will not only stick but also turn into future sales, many referrals, and a stronger relationship between you.

1. Congratulate them.

Be happy for them and show it. Focus on them, not you. They already know you're happy for yourself. Example: "I am so happy for you. Congratulations on buying this particular model."

2. Point to the future.

The moment they buy, strengthen their decision by pointing to their future use of the product or service. Example: "With this service, I think you'll find that X happens easier for you."

3. Ask why they bought.

This is good for them to tell what made the difference. You'll learn a lot, too. For example: "John, may I ask why you chose the Chevy Blazer today?"

4. Offer to answer more questions.

Previously their questions were about gathering information. Now, their questions are about owning the product. Example: "Now that you're the proud owner of this Maserati, what questions can I answer for you?"

5. Tell them what's next.

Lay out the next steps that they or you will be taking. If they balk you can probably resolve it now. Example: "Great, Karen. Now I will . . ."

6. Tell them what you are going to do for them.

This will reassure them and put you in control. Example: "There are three things I'm going to do for you in the next week. . . ."

7. Get the payment.

People vote more with their money than with their words. Example: "How did you want to handle the purchase?" Or, the classic, "Will that be on your credit card?"

8. Get permission to contact them in 30 days.

Doing this lets them know that you'll be calling them, which reinforces their decision to buy and opens the door for great service and referrals. Example: "Susan, I usually ask my customers if I can call them in about a month to hear how they are enjoying their new computer and see if I can answer any questions that come up between now and then."

9. Ferret out any unspoken concerns or doubts.

We all have doubts about almost everything we buy. Going the extra mile here may lose you a sale from time to time, but usually it improves your reputation and strengthens the sale and customer satisfaction level. Example: "Do you have any doubts about this purchase that I can help you with?"

10. Prepare them for reactions that they may have in the next month about using the product or service.

The more you can inform the new customer about what they might experience or what might happen when using their new purchase, the more they will trust you and the less severe the reaction will be if it does occur. Example: "May I let you know what I've heard that my other customers experienced in the first month of using the same high-end computer system?"

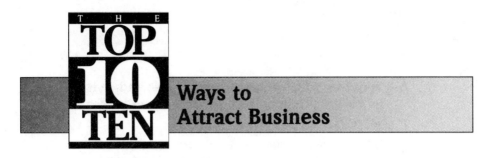

Ways to Attract Business

1. Be a walking example of how effective your product or service is.

2. Seek to serve instead of just seeking to sell.

3. Add value by networking all of the time: Be a matchmaker every single day.

4. Add value to your potential customers by expanding their professional vision and goals.

5. Add value to your current customers by making sure they're making the best use of your product or service.

6. Turn your customers into your company's research and development department, not just a focus group.

7. Improve your communication skills and style of relating to people so that they *want* to be around you—a lot!

8. Turn your customers into your sales deputies; have them feed you business instead of you having to "prospect" for it.

9. Teach others how to sell in an irresistibly attractive way; this guarantees you a strong future.

10. Strengthen your personal financial portfolio so you don't *need* the money anymore.

Ways to Get the Most out of Your PR Firm

Public relations firms live in a world of hype, and often start believing how good they are and how hard they are working for you. Don't buy that; make them prove it. The following tips, learned the hard way, should help.

1. Make them promise specific results or specific actions.

2. Have them deliver a ten-point report each week.

3. Identify, in advance, the placements you're looking for.

4. Have the firm upgrade your media kit.

5. Tell the firm how you want each media placement leveraged.

6. Create a list of ten strong angles for your campaign.

7. Warn the PR firm that they'll be fired if X doesn't happen.

8. Work only with the *best* people in the firm. No rookies.

9. Ask the *reporters* what they thought of your firm's professionalism.

10. Review results every 30 days; insist on this meeting.

Keys to a Strong International Marketing Plan

1. Know your target market.

Select your market (country) based on the need you perceive for your product in that market. To find out if there is a need for your product there are several sources you can tap. (1) The country's embassy or consulate. Embassies are generally in Washington, D.C. Depending on the size of the country, consulates are located in major or strategic cities around the United States. (2) The local library. If your library is on-line, it might have access to a National Trade Data Base (NTDB), which is updated monthly. You can also subscribe to the NTDB service and receive a monthly CD-ROM.

2. Know your competition.

Determine your domestic competitors. What are their distributors or sales outlets in your target country? Determine local competitors in the target country and find out where their products originate. Access pricing information if you can. Again, embassies and consulates as well as that country's trade mission (if any) and their chamber of commerce (here and local) may be helpful.

3. Move cautiously into new markets.

The decision to market in a new country has far-reaching effects on product development, pricing, finances, and staffing. Do you need to conform to special laws and standards (such as ISO 9000, metric measurements, and so on)? Does your product come under export restrictions (strategic high tech products)? Does your product require specially trained technical support?

Do you need to translate documentation? (Warning! Translations need to be done in the translator's native language and he or she must be familiar with your industry.)

4. Should you use a distributor or your own sales force?

Using your own sales reps means they are your employees and therefore you determine the scope of their sales efforts. It also gives you "presence" in that country. The downside is that it is expensive—you pay them whether you sell anything or not. Unless you are there physically you don't really have control over their activities. Distributors, in contrast, are established companies with their own presence, infrastructure, and track record. They are already staffed, have a grasp of the market, and they may have already a pipeline of prospects for your product. The downside is that they usually represent many other products as well.

5. Choose a distributor intelligently.

The U.S. embassy in your target country can help locate potential distributors for you. There is a fee associated with that; check with the Department of Commerce (DOC). You can also check trade directories for the region (where available) and local trade publications for ads from distributors. You may want to ask another company that has similar products to yours (but not competitive) and find out who their distributor is. Check the native embassy or consulate for directories as well. After you contact potential distributors find out who they represent, how many products are in their line, how many sales reps they have, what their annual volume is, what they feel the market for your product might be, and if they have technical support staff (if required for your product). When you have interviewed several potential distributors (on the phone, fax, or e-mail), spend the money and visit the country and meet them personally.

6. Craft legal agreements carefully.

It is of utmost importance that you execute a distributorship agreement (or sales rep agreement) which has been reviewed by an attorney with international contract experience. It should contain, in addition to the boiler plate clauses, length of term, the distributor's disclosure restrictions, pricing policies, discount policies, technical support policies, staff training, customer training, who pays for documentation expenses, translations (if applicable), commissions and royalties, and sales quotas. If a distributor wants and gets exclusive geographic rights, then quota requirements are a must. If the distributor does not make quota for a specified number of times, he should lose the distributorship or the exclusive status. Establish policy on multinational accounts, "house" accounts, third-party sales, and so on.

7. Establish support guidelines.

You have to consider what kind of support your distributor or sales rep will get. If it is an "easy" product, there may be very little technical support required. High-tech products like hardware and software require skilled technical support not only from you to the distributor but also from the distributor to the customer. A representative from your distributor should attend training at your headquarters, or you need to provide that training on-site. Specify in your agreement who pays for this training.

8. Establish what the potential market for your product is.

Although ample market research may be available, you may have to do some local research yourself. What is the "life" of your product? Is it something consumers will purchase on a long-term continual basis or is it a seasonal product or fad? Is it a capital purchase which requires regular maintenance long term? Is there residual income from maintenance, support, or value-added services?

9. Consider the cost of marketing overseas.

If you decide to market in one country, determine how much more expensive it would be to market to a number of countries in the same region. Factor the cost of travel and related expenses, regional and local trade shows, local training, documentation, translations, added technical and other support, communication costs (telephone and fax), licensing (export and local), and adaptation to local standards and laws (i.e., 220V/50Hz).

10. Make a long-term commitment.

The decision to sell a product in foreign markets is a long-term commitment. The first 12 to 18 months are difficult at best and most likely will not show a profit. Your company and product must build a customer confidence, which takes time. When building a marketing plan, project sales and cost figures for at least five years, and update them regularly. A comprehensive business plan is essential.

Ways to Get Big-Time Media Coverage

1. Write a book on something you like or do—become an instant expert.

2. Challenge an existing institution and show that you're making progress.

3. Create a way to do something with 10 percent less time or cost.

4. Create a Web site or e-mail newsletter and wait for a reporter to start your media coverage.

5. Hire a PR firm and ask *them* to get coverage for you.

6. Build a track record of serving a particular niche and then call your local newspaper, tell your story, and see if they're interested.

7. Take an existing product or service, and customize it so that it's revolutionary.

8. Link what you offer to an already existing trend or news event.

9. Add an electronic or free component to what you offer and pitch the story with an Internet angle.

10. Get someone well-known to endorse you or what you're offering.

Components for Every 60-Second Sales Pitch

1. Name of the company or product.

2. Name of the buyer.

3. Primary benefit that the buyer receives *if* they buy the product.

4. Instructions on how to get that benefit.

5. Ask for the order.

6. Be positive and excited about your product. Demonstrate confidence.

7. Inform the buyer how this product will better position them in the world.

8. Identify and fill at least one hole or need of the buyer.

9. Authenticity (be honest, cleanspoken and *real,* not "salesy").

10. Treat the buyers as if they *are* going to buy instead of waiting for them to say yes.

2

ENTREPRENEURSHIP

Mistakes Most Entrepreneurs Make

1. Getting wedded to an idea and sticking with it too long.

Don't marry a single idea. Remember, ideas are the currency of entrepreneurs. Play with many ideas and see which ones bring money and success.

2. Trying to be something other than an entrepreneur.

Entrepreneurs are entrepreneurs. You'll give yourself a hernia if you try to act like other people. Your difference is your strength.

3. Believing your own spin.

Entrepreneurs are genetically wired to be optimistic. Just don't believe everything you say to others.

4. Ignoring your cash position.

The world doesn't respond even to superior products in the time frame that you think they should. You'll need plenty of cash to sustain yourself in the meantime.

5. Attracting weak staff members.

Not that many great employees will put up with a mercurial or childish/immature entrepreneur. If you're attracting weak people, you'll need to mature as a human being.

6. Confusing possibility with reality.

The successful entrepreneur lives in a world of possibility but spends money in the world of reality.

7. Selling too hard.

If you find yourself selling an idea or product too hard to too many people, perhaps it's time to listen to why they are not buying and learn from that instead of trying to become a better salesperson.

8. Not setting up support structures.

Hire people and services to handle many of your business and personal needs. Most entrepreneurs do better when they are fully supported, even if transparently.

9. Over-delegating.

Most entrepreneurs over-delegate tasks and accountabilities to others, also known as "dumping." It's far better to learn how to delegate rather than dump; that is, give others the information they need to do the job, then get out of the way.

10. Giving up.

Some of the most successful entrepreneurs failed several times before doing extremely well. So, if you're failing, fail. And fail fast. And learn. And try again, with this new wisdom. Do not give up.

THE

TOP 10 TEN

Great Qualities That Cause the Most Problems

Entrepreneurs, like any pioneers, have their own sets of (always evolving) rules and strategies. Many entrepreneurs are successful in spite of themselves. The key to working with entrepreneurs is to understand their weaknesses, because these are often their biggest strengths, although *you* may not think so!

1. Entrepreneurs can't focus, have lots of ideas, but run in circles.

If entrepreneurs could focus, they'd be bookkeepers (no offense to bookkeepers; I was a CPA for years). The entrepreneur's currency is ideas, often a flood of ideas. This is good. Encourage more ideas; don't try to pin them down. When you challenge them to come up with more and better ideas—instead of pressuring them to focus on just one—the flow is restored and they'll find the one they should focus on. Really. The reason they can't focus is that they haven't yet flushed out all of the half-baked ones.

2. Entrepreneurs are not good with details.

Why should they be? Sure, it would great if they would focus on details, but given that many don't deal with details well, suggest they give up even trying. Sure, this may create a mess, but challenge the entrepreneur to solve the mess as if the mess was a new business! That'll get 'em thinking! (Entrepreneurs are like kids; it's good to divert them.)

3. Entrepreneurs feel odd, different, alone, strange.

Entrepreneurs are simply wired differently and they should feel this way, because it's true. There's nothing wrong with that. In fact, if you can help the entrepreneur to relish their unique, contrary, leading-edge ways, you'll help them feel better about themselves, which will increase the flow of ideas and success. Educate the entrepreneur to understand not just themselves as individuals but to understand about the species called homo entrepreneuris.

4. Entrepreneurs are good at starting businesses, but bad at running them.

Many entrepreneurs think they have an obligation to run their businesses and become great managers. Most never will be great managers; they shouldn't even try. The solution: Help the entrepreneur to set a "sell date" right now, so they know they're getting out and when. This relieves some of the pressure and also forces the entrepreneur to create a saleable company instead of one that is just a monument to their ego (and I mean this lovingly). Selling is not failure; it's good business and lets the entrepreneur play instead of being saddled with responsibilities and accountabilities that he doesn't really want.

5. Chaos reigns in an entrepreneur's company.

The entrepreneur likes chaos and is unlikely to hire a manager that is cross-platform: able to both manage the people and operations and also able to put up with the personality or constant flow of ideas and changes that the entrepreneur is likely to have. A solution is to design the company so that it can afford the chaos and the financial stress that chaos usually brings. Another solution is to ask the entrepreneur to solve the chaos problem by thinking of it as a foundering business that the entrepreneur has purchased. This will get the juices flowing. Yet another solution is to help the entrepreneur create fully automated and foolproof systems, usually managed by outside contractors or vendors who are not in the business day to day.

6. Entrepreneurs fail. And fail again.

Just like a kid has to fall a couple of times when learning to ride a bike, so do entrepreneurs fail as they learn how to be successful. Remember, it's the spark that the entrepreneur has that is the real source of profitability. It's just that there is often a learning curve as entrepreneurs learn to compensate for their weaknesses by delegating, outsourcing, maturing, and learning new skills. The spark usually wins in the end.

7. Entrepreneurs exaggerate and are too optimistic.

This is good! Encourage entrepreneurs to exaggerate as much they want. This is a reverse way to get them to tell the truth. It works. Entrepreneurs are so out in front of the rest of us that they need to exaggerate how well things are going, in order to keep the faith. Many entrepreneurs grow through this, but don't try to take away their security blanket until they're ready. They need it.

8. Entrepreneurs are always on the edge financially.

This one's a toughie, because of the "unnecessary" stress it can cause to the entrepreneur, the business, employees, and families. The entrepreneur who is always at the edge is using the business to heal an emotional dilemma. This may be an addiction to adrenaline, the pleasure of "pulling it off" at the last minute, the high that victory brings, the need to be better than everyone else, and even the inability to establish a reserve of cash and time so that they function without this stress. But despite the problems it can create, being at the edge financially really is a strength. Through this mechanism, entrepreneurs have proven, time and time again, that they are resourceful and can survive and bounce back from adversity. Now, help the entrepreneur to direct this energy into creating a healthy savings account instead of leveraging so much, and you'll have a successful entrepreneur.

9. The families of entrepreneurs suffer.

Another toughie. You didn't just marry a person or even a businessperson. You married an entrepreneur! And that entrepreneur didn't come with instructions, warning labels, or antidotes. It's best that you develop your own strong interests and let your spouse do their own thing. You'll always be #2 (well, maybe #1 ½). You can have a great marriage if you understand this.

10. Sales often dip in entrepreneurial companies.

Sales dip because the entrepreneurs turn over some or all of the sales function to others. Take this as an invitation for entrepreneurs to get back to selling, where they usually shine.

Components of a Winning Business Plan

1. Why do you need a business plan?

Would you go on a long trip without a map? No. The same logic applies in business. You need to map out the path for your company's growth, set goals and targets, and determine the things you need on your journey to success.

2. Prepare for the financiers.

If you need financing, you won't get it without a good business plan. Banks want to see it, investors want to see it, venture capitalists want to see it.

3. Establish a yardstick.

You'll need some type of tool to measure where you are on your journey to success and how you are doing based on your goals and targets.

4. Use all your resources to develop a business plan.

Visit the library. There are literally tons of books with good stuff in them on business plans. There may be some variances in the different books, but overall they say the same thing. Just get started and use the books as guides, not as absolutes.

5. Write an executive summary.

This should be your cover page—the big headline so to speak. It should be contained to one page—two at most—and include your business objectives, a description of your business, your market and business opportunity, and the financial highlights (primarily, how much money will you need?).

6. Present a financial plan.

It should contain the following items in detail: (1) projected sales and revenues, (2) projected net profits, (3) projected cash flow, (4) break-even analysis, (5) pay-back period, (6) main sensitivity analysis, and (7) financial requirements. These projections should be month by month for the first 12 months, then quarterly for the next five years. Prepare the following pro forma reports for the next 3–5 years: (1) profit and loss, (2) cash flow, (3) balance sheet, and (4) operational budget. Provide explanations of your financial assumptions.

7. What goes between the executive summary and the financial plan?

Present your plans for the following components: (1) the company history to date, (2) products and services, (3) market analysis, (4) marketing strategy and plan, (5) research and development plan (if applicable), (6) management and organization, (7) operating plan, and (8) facilities and equipment (if applicable). Provide sufficient detail for an uninitiated reader to understand. Use short, plain language. Use brochures, drawings, sketches, etc., as appropriate to illustrate.

8. Read it again, and have someone else read it.

When you have a draft of your business plan, give it to several trusted people to proofread with instructions to consider: (1) spelling and grammar, (2) ease of reading and clarity, (3) completeness of content, (4) accuracy of the numbers.

9. Polish your presentation.

Get it word processed and print it on high-quality paper. Have at least two more people proofread the near-final copy. Make several high-quality photocopies of your entire plan (depending on whether you'll be sending it out for financing or not), and keep the original for yourself for further copying. Choose a nice presentation folder. The cover sheet should only read: "Business Plan of [your name]" and the date.

10. Now what?

Hopefully, you have been investigating your financing prospects. The time has come to send out your plan. Usually, the initial contact with an investor or financial institution is only the executive summary. Don't send out the entire business plan until you know that you have an interested party and not just a tire kicker. A brief, professional letter should accompany your summary. Good luck!

THE TOP 10 TEN

Phrases Entrepreneurs Use That Limit Their Success

1. "When I . . ."

Uh, huh.

2. "If I can do X, then Y will result . . ."

Big if.

3. "It should . . ."

Yeah, it should, but will it?

4. "I could . . ."

Yes, but will you?

5. "If I could just . . ."

Nah; it ain't that easy.

6. "It's a done deal . . ."

It ain't really done until the client's check has been cashed and the services or goods have been delivered.

7. "We're very close . . ."

Close to what—reality? Dream on.

8. "If only . . ."

If only pigs could fly.

9. "If you'd just support me . . ."

Support yourself.

10. "No one understands what I am trying to do . . ."

Very likely, but that means you're really an entrepreneur.
If they did understand, you wouldn't have much to offer, then,
would you?

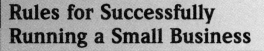

THE TOP 10 TEN
Rules for Successfully Running a Small Business

You've just been in a serious car accident, and you'll have to be out of the office at least a month. How will your business run while you recover? If you've just experienced heart failure over this prospect, the following list is for you. The information below can reduce your stress, increase your business's productivity, and give you the time for the vacation you so richly deserve.

1. Hire wisely.

Your business is only as good as each individual employee's contribution to it. Therefore, look for the three I's when you hire: intelligence, initiative, and integrity. For every position, from receptionist to packing clerk, hire only the best you can find.

2. Build a team, not your ego.

Many employers let their egos dominate their interactions with their employees. Stop the pattern. Instead, trust your employees to do their jobs. Let all your employees know they are an integral part of the company's end product. Set the example for positive interaction at all times between members of the team, even when their performance must be corrected.

3. Reward good employees well.

When you find good employees, reward them financially and emotionally. Pay them well, but also take time to acknowledge each employee's contribution. The two biggest loyalty builders are the words "thank you."

4. Be "hands on."

Know each employee's job and how to do it. This not only gives you an automatic reserve employee and trainer (yourself), but has an added bonus. If you show employees that you are willing to learn their jobs, you are letting them know that you believe their work has value.

5. Encourage your employees to be versatile.

In a small company, every employee should know how to do at least two jobs, particularly on the technical and service sides. For critical tasks, at least three employees should know how to do each job. Then you always have an on-the-premises reserve who can step in when needed.

6. Give away tasks, but not ultimate leadership.

What is it you do best? Are you the idea man, the best salesman in your company, the organizer? Find your strongest talent and then delegate all other tasks to your employees. Train them to do their jobs, let them know you have confidence in their ability to perform, and then let them do their jobs. At the same time, you must remain in charge.

7. Communicate, communicate, communicate— did we mention communicate?

You must talk with your employees, solicit their suggestions, and correct their mistakes in a positive way. Conversely, you must create an atmosphere in which employees are willing to talk with you. The two best sources of information on your business are your employees and your customers. Pay attention to both.

8. Give your best and always encourage the same in your employees.

Pride in the company and its product or service always begins at the top. If you give a half effort or let a sloppily produced product go out the door, you are sending a message to your employees that you do not respect your clients or your work. Your employees will adopt that view as well. On the other hand, if you set the example of giving the extra effort, and working as a unit to be the best in the business, your employees will follow your lead.

9. Encourage innovation and creation.

Give your employees a stake in the future. Once a month, have a meeting where the employees make suggestions on how to improve your product, service, efficiency, or bottom line. Give monetary rewards when the ideas pay off.

10. Have a second in command.

No general goes into battle without a major who can take over if he is wounded. Find someone you trust within your company who shares your goals, ideals, and business style. Train that person appropriately. Let others know that your "major" has your confidence and authority when you are gone. When that is done, leave on vacation and test the theory out. If you have completed steps 1–9 above, your business will run easily and well and you will have regained a healthy balance in your life.

Reasons to Keep Your Job While Starting a New Business

1. Contacts

Your current work environment probably gives you immediate access to lots of people (prospective customers, experts, support). You lose some of this when you quit.

2. Cash flow

Every entrepreneur is optimistic; your business will take twice as long as you think to become profitable. Keep the job cash coming in, even if it appears "so small" compared to what you "plan" to be making.

3. Momentum

Most work environments provide a pace, a routine, a flow. You'll lose this quickly when you're on your own.

4. Support

Better to start your business while still working at a straight job, because you really need the love and support that coworkers can provide, given that starting a small business is really stressful and often fear-producing.

5. Integrity

Keeping the paycheck coming in is the right thing to do unless you have two to three years of cash in the bank. The moment you put yourself at needless financial risk, you'll likely attract nasty surprises and setbacks. Not fair, but often true.

6. Equipment

Often, you can use the software, computers, copy machines, faxes, etc., at your office, thus saving you money as you start up your company.

7. Time to test out your product or service

Most businesses fail, so don't think that you're bigger than the statistics! Give yourself plenty of time to experiment, test, and improve your idea or product to the point that it sells itself. You need time to make your product or service that viable.

8. Networking opportunities

Now that you know you're going to start a business, every meeting, conference, or get-together now serves two purposes— your straight job and your new business.

9. Structure

Sometimes, you need the structure of your regular job to help you make the transition to the self-structuring of your entrepreneurial job.

10. Inside information

It's much easier to stay in touch with industry and the business world from within a big company than from within a start-up organization. Larger companies have access to much more information than one-horse organizations do. You may need that information.

Questions to Ask When Reviewing a Business Plan

1. What is the track record of the principals involved? How much experience and character do they have?

2. What are the five external events or factors that could put this proposed company out of business quickly?

3. Will the proposed company be able to pay off their financing early? How early?

4. Is the proposed company taking full advantage of administrative and production automation?

5. How committed are the principals to immediate and consistent cash flow and profitability versus just revenue growth and market share?

6. Would I put my children's education fund into this deal?

7. How flexible, responsive, customer-oriented, and creative are the principals?

8. Are they trying to impress me or putting a too-positive spin in this proposal, or are they being straight?

9. What are the weird feelings, inklings, red flags, inconsistencies, unclear points that I am noticing?

10. Why do they need so much money? How could they get started on a shoe-string basis instead?

3

**CUSTOMER
SERVICE**

Ways to Get Disgruntled or Past Customers Back

1. Offer them a complete refund, free upgrade, a replacement—whatever it takes.

2. Ask them to join your Quality Assurance Team.

3. Prove to them that their input about their problem has measurably changed how you do business.

4. Give them your direct line to handle future problems or complaints.

5. Admit the problem as a *problem,* rather than just something that *they* experienced.

6. Show them the facts, figures, statistics, or trends that demonstrate that their bad experience was an exception.

7. Ask them what they would like from you if they were to come back as a customer.

8. Hire them!

9. Ask them to join your board of directors or advisors or research and development team.

10. Ask for their forgiveness.

Ways to Turn Your Customers into Raving Fans

1. Be someone that they really enjoy as a person and as a vendor.

2. Call your customers each quarter to ask if they're having any problems or have ideas for improvement.

3. Continually improve your product.

4. Keep your customers informed about future changes and upgrades for the product they bought.

5. Keep your customers informed about what the media and other customers are saying about what they bought.

6. Keep your customers completely informed when there's a problem or perceived problem about your product.

7. Educate your customers on making the most of your product.

8. Do the unexpected, again and again.

9. Create a "special client-only" club that gets extra things, early announcements, special invitations—anything worthwhile.

10. Be six to twenty-four months ahead of the competition—and stay there.

THE TOP 10 TEN

Ways to Put Your Best Public Foot Forward

1. Hire a great receptionist.

In 90 percent of all cases, a person's first contact with your business occurs when your receptionist answers the phone. In addition, your receptionist will greet all of your customers and clients every time they walk in the door. Most organizations, however, look at receptionists as the low rung on the ladder, pay the position barely more than minimum wage, and then wonder why they have an unending stream of bad receptionists who create a poor first impression. Give priority to hiring a bright, friendly, energetic, well-mannered, and unflappable person for the job and then pay enough to keep that person for a long time.

2. Train your receptionist to direct people appropriately.

Your receptionist should be more than a greeter. He or she should be able to instantly direct clients and customers to whomever can best serve their needs. Therefore, be sure your receptionist is thoroughly familiar with the work that each company member does and what types of clients or customers each work with. In addition, your receptionist should have a list of key referrals. This will let the public know immediately that yours is an efficient organization catering to client and customer needs. Finally, your receptionist should never be eating lunch or reading a magazine at the front desk. Find other more productive tasks for the times when the phone is not ringing.

3. Keep your voice mail to a minimum.

While voice mail has been a technological blessing, make no mistake about it—the public hates voice mail. Every client and customer will tell you the same thing: each wants to talk to a real person who can solve their problem as soon as possible. Therefore, keep all voice mail brief and informative, and only use it when your receptionist is unavailable or your office is closed. It should concisely state the name of your business, your office hours, and welcome the caller to leave a message or call back during regular business hours. It should also give your fax number for those wishing to send a fax. If you are using voice mail frequently during the day, then you do not have enough phone lines and you should make arrangements to add additional lines. If your staff has voice mail, it should be changed daily and briefly state when the staff member will be in the office and reachable. It should also invite the caller to leave a message or return to the operator. Always give the caller the option to speak to someone real. Again, this says "We care about serving you" more than any voice mail message does.

4. Maintain a clean and attractive lobby.

You do not need fancy offices with expensive furniture and artwork to impress the public. In fact, many members of the public know that such overhead is worked into the monthly fee and would prefer not to be paying for your artwork. A lobby needs only a few things to make a good first impression: attractive furniture, good lighting, clean carpet, a few green plants, and some good prints on the walls. Provide magazines that are informative, but not gossipy. Finally, be sure there is some literature, such as a brochure, that tells what you do and how well you do it. The client or customer can then learn about your business before he or she ever shakes your hand.

5. Keep your halls clean, attractive, and uncluttered.

Hallways are not storage areas, no matter how short on space you are. Again, be sure your carpet is clean and not well worn. Add some inexpensive, but tasteful prints to the walls. Remember that your clients and customers will walk down these hallways every time they see you, so the hallways are as important as the lobby space.

6. Insist that all of your staff in every position keep a clean desk and office.

Your client has walked through your attractive lobby and halls. The client now walks into Jane Smith's office and sees a desk littered with paper, files everywhere, and Jane has to hunt for a pad and pen to begin taking notes on what the client needs. Is your client impressed? No. Is your client confident that Jane can take care of his or her needs in an orderly and efficient manner? Absolutely not. Will your client remember Jane's disorganization when she neglects to adequately serve him or her? You bet. Therefore, instill in each staff member that their office is a reflection of the respect they accord their clients, customers, and themselves. Your public image will not only grow, but your staff will be more productive as well.

7. Develop a simple staff dress code that reflects your service.

Make sure your employees know what dress is expected of them.

8. Make your office a pleasant place to work.

Clients and customers immediately sense if there's tension in the air. Moreover, an unhappy employee, let alone several, will never convey a positive image for your business. Therefore, take reasonable steps to be sure your staff both enjoys and takes pride in their work. The president or manager should provide the staff with positive reinforcement on a regular basis and good work should be rewarded both financially and emotionally for its contribution to the company's success. These efforts will produce employees who quite naturally convey a positive image for the company and easily attract and keep clients and customers.

9. Your letterhead should reflect your professionalism.

Again, fancy is not necessary or necessarily better. A service organization should convey that they simply and efficiently respond to a client's needs. Letterhead and business cards, therefore, don't need complex logos or gold embossed printing. Instead, use a good stationery stock. Cheap paper will communicate that you cut corners with quality. Then, use a standard ink color such as black, navy, brown, or burgundy. Your letterhead must tell a client how to reach you. It should contain your company's name, address, phone, fax, and e-mail address. If you have a Web page, your Web address should appear as well. Keep logos simple so that they don't overwhelm the information about who you are and what you do.

10. Follow up with great service.

No initial public impression lasts for long. Whether your business or organization maintains a positive impression depends on the service delivered to each customer. Therefore, anticipate your customers' needs and fulfill them before they are stated.

Add value to your service on a regular basis. Most importantly, communicate constantly with your clients and customers. Return phone calls within 24 hours. Inform them when something important has occurred which impacts the client and the client's business. Think about the professional who serves you best and emulate that service to your clients and customers. Your clients will then augment your first impression by their last impression: a service organization that not only serves, but serves well. As a result, you will find your business growing and prospering.

Customer Satisfaction Audit Questions

1. How do we define customer satisfaction?

2. How much should we be spending on retaining customers?

3. Why do customers defect?

4. What report or measurable goal do we need weekly to track our progress in this area?

5. What are the needs that our customers haven't even asked us to fulfill for them?

6. How rapidly are customer questions and problems resolved?

7. Do customer questions or complaints get forwarded to our product team?

8. Are our customers delighted or just satisfied?

9. Do our customers brag to their friends about our product or service?

10. If we were the customer, where would we ask the company to improve?

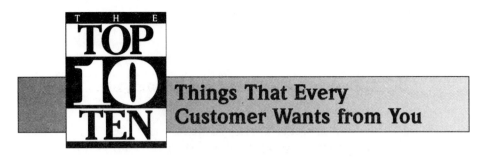

THE TOP 10 TEN

Things That Every Customer Wants from You

1. They want it to cost less money, even if it's already value-priced.

2. They want it to act faster—immediately.

3. They want it to come to them or be delivered.

4. They want it to be replenished/updated/upgraded/replaced automatically and consistently.

5. They want it even before they know it's available or that they even need or want it.

6. They want it pre-customized to fit their unique needs.

7. They want it to come pre-assembled and ready to run—no instructions or thinking needed.

8. They want to be able to return it with no hassle: a solid/flexible guarantee.

9. They want it to work perfectly and beyond all expectations.

10. They want to feel good about using your product and being a customer of yours.

Ways to Turn Your Good Clients into Your Best Clients

What if every client could be your best client? Yes, it's possible. Here are some tips on how to do just that.

1. **Let them know that you want them to become your best client.**

2. **When they are not acting as if they were your best client, ask them to change immediately.**

3. **Identify the tools that they need to get on track to becoming your best customer.**

4. **Provide these tools and instruct the client in using them most effectively.**

5. **Treat the client as if they *are* your best client and they'll respond accordingly.**

6. **Remind them how special, good, successful, and bright they are.**

7. Identify the behaviors or attitudes that prevent them from being your best client and help the client to fix these.

8. If a client doesn't want to be on this track, let them go if they are draining you.

9. Find a way to introduce your best clients to each other and watch them all become even *better* best clients!

10. Want more for your clients than even they can conceive of and let this vision affect how you serve them.

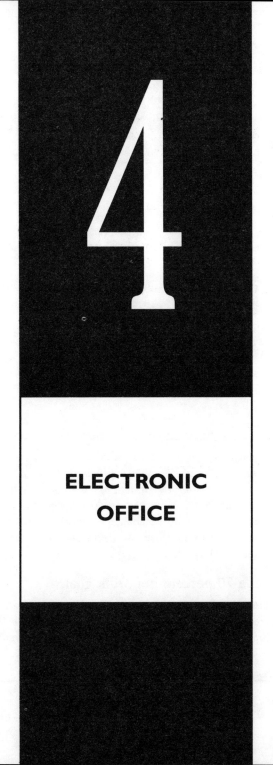

4

ELECTRONIC OFFICE

Keys to Running a Highly Profitable Virtual Company

A "virtual" company delivers services and products via the Internet or other electronic means.

1. Accept the fact that virtual companies will rule.

The most profound, underlying trend in the world today is the eradication of wasteful and inefficient ways of doing business. Occupancy costs, service personnel, and a sales force are examples of expenses that are on their way out. Those companies that reengineer how they market and deliver goods and services will survive, the rest will fold. Why? Because customers simply won't pay the extra premium.

2. Become fully automated, not just virtual.

You want one million customers to be able to buy from you without having to speak to a single person via phone or e-mail. The best customers don't even want to talk to anybody, they want your product or service to be clearly described and simple to order. To become fully automated means that you design Web-based, real-time systems to handle virtually all the needs of your potential customers.

3. Set a 70 percent net profit goal.

Just by setting such an aggressive goal, you'll feel pressed to create radical new ways to run the business, and the 70 percent profit goal will filter out the "good ideas" that just aren't good enough. This goal will also filter out the normal inclination to solve problems and customer needs in the old fashioned, non-virtual way.

4. Repackage, reprice, or reposition what you currently sell so that 100 million people can buy it.

Isn't it worth reexamining what you sell in order to appeal to 100 million potential customers now and one billion Internet customers within a few years?

5. Find ways to be in frequent, personal touch with current and potential customers.

The personal touch can be electronic, really! Personal means that you have created ways to offer customers value by standing in their shoes and offering them what they most need, even before they know what that is. That's personal! Use newsletters, customer-only specials, and free trial offers to connect to customers on a personal level.

6. Learn from your potential customers what they want you to do differently.

A benefit of being virtual is that customers feel free to tell you honestly how they feel about your company and what they want from it, thanks to the safety of the distance provided by the Internet. But you have to ask and keep asking. We call this an "interdevelopmental relationship."

7. Customize and repackage what you offer to appeal to as many niches or needs as you can.

The future of consumerism is in customized products and services. And, thanks to the Internet, you'll be able to find customers for special needs far faster than via traditional marketing methods. If you create it and the public wants it, they can and will find you!

8. Accept the fact that information longs to be free and eventually will be.

This is an inescapable trend. If you're charging for information now, you won't be able to within a decade. So, loosen up and give away what you can, and find ways to package what's left to be extremely valuable to your customers; they'll pay you well for it.

9. Systematize all that you do, so that you're freed up to respond to what's new.

Your future profits likely will come from a different source than today's profits. Just make sure that you've got the time and the space to grasp where the future of your business is. If you're too busy administering and managing, you'll miss the future!

10. Create a profile of your ideal customer of today, not your ideal customer of yesterday.

You can reach very different customers today, thanks to the Internet. Identify them now and reorient your company around serving them, even if it means that you'll take the focus away from your current customer base. Remember, there will soon be a two-class society—those with Internet access and those without. Don't be caught serving the clients who aren't up to speed electronically.

Ways to Go Paperless and Administration Free

1. Change your mailing address to that of your accountant/bill-paying service.

2. Use only a credit card or debit card for all purchases.

3. Arrange for a bill-paying service or accountant that uses Quicken and CheckFree.

4. Use a scanner.

5. Have a virtual assistant who handles everything for you.

6. Arrange for all food and other home supplies to be delivered instead of shopping for them.

7. Simplify your life.

8. Get on the Internet.

9. Buy software that can automate things for you.

10. Set up electronic, automated reminders for important dates and events.

THE TOP 10 TEN

Virtual Management Skills

With virtual management skills, you can manage others or projects without being physically present. This skill set is becoming increasingly valued in the marketplace because of the leverage, immediacy, and cost savings of highly effective virtual managers.

1. Conduct group teleconference meetings instead of traveling.

There is a unique set of skills to learn that make these tele-meetings highly effective—and keep you from spending all your time traveling.

2. Use group teleclasses to train employees.

Use these to conduct training over the phone instead of on site. You can spend your time training instead of traveling.

3. Create just-in-time training modules.

Offer these via a Web site, e-mail, fax on demand, or tele-conference call to provide immediate training and solutions to staff who are facing similar problems.

4. Learn to use e-mail effectively.

The highly effective virtual manager responds to between 50 and 200 e-mail messages a day. Learning the ins and outs of e-mail software, autoresponders and e-mailing lists will reduce by at least 50 percent the time you spend answering e-mail.

5. Use voice-mail to stay informed without having to take all those calls.

Set up a call-in system so your folks in the field can call in their results as they occur instead of waiting for a meeting or taking dozens of calls personally. This keeps everyone on their toes but also keeps you informed the moment things are happening.

6. Use pagers to stay in touch.

Send out messages (e-mail, alphanumeric, or text) throughout the day to keep everyone updated and motivated.

7. Turn your Web site or Intranet into a tool for sharing information within the company.

Web sites are now also becoming stations for gathering data. Rather than having the branch managers send e-mail or write up text reports, they can just go to the company's Web site and key into a predesigned form that will then forward the information to a database and generate a report to the virtual manager. Sure reduces the number of e-mails flying around!

8. Learn to use project management software to stay on top things.

There are several good packages available that help the virtual manager keep in touch with all aspects of a project.

9. Find groupware that can help the whole team work together better.

Groupware is collaboration and tracking software (like Lotus Notes) that lets everyone on the team communicate directly with other members (and with you as virtual manager) without having to talk with them or be at the same place at the same time.

10. Establish clear goals and a vision.

What is the glue that keeps the team working even when you're not physically present? Usually it's a great goal, shared vision, or game plan that keeps everyone focused and excited. This, plus the tools and techniques described above, makes virtual management work well.

THE
TOP
10
TEN

Interactive Features for a Hot Web Site

You will attract a more apprecia-
tive audience if you can provide some interactive content at your
Web site.

1. Register to receive something valuable.

*Let your visitors register their names and leave comments about
your site. But don't ask them to sign the guest book without
giving them something—a subscription to your newsletter,
some pithy wisdom, or something of value to them.*

2. Respond to your content.

*Invite your visitors to let you know what they think about your
Web site.*

3. Fill out an order form.

Let your visitors order a product or service of value to them.

4. Perform a self-assessment.

*Your visitors might enjoy filling out a quiz and receiving an instant
response with an interpretation of their results.*

5. Get access to a resource directory.

*Provide a database of resources and a search engine to allow
visitors to locate a resource description. It could be a reading list,
a list of recommended videos, or just about anything else.*

6. Take advantage of a matching service.

Provide a place for people to register and match themselves with others. Similar to the "Companions 2 Travel" Web site (www.companions2travel.com) and the "Coach Referral Service" (www.coachreferral.com).

7. Chat about topics that interest them.

You might enjoy hosting a Web discussion group on a special interest topic.

8. Take advantage of interactive e-mail.

Take your autoresponder to a new level. Provide resources through e-mail requests that generate searches or provide selectable information. Send an e-mail to index@topten.org for an example of resources available on request to coaches.

9. Enter a creation contest.

Host a creation site for special interests. Invite visitors to create the content of your site, complete with automatically generated Web pages, indexes, and search engines.

10. Discover your site's artificial intelligence.

Use the Web as a front-end to your knowledge base.

THE TOP 10 TEN

Distinctions to Grasp When Building a Web Site

Creating a home page or full Web site is as much an investment in your own training and skill set as it is a marketing step. The purpose of this list is to expand your thinking and help you to get your arms around the key elements of Web site design.

1. Resource center vs. Billboard.

Many home pages and Web sites are simply electronic billboards or brochures. This is better than nothing, but successful Web sites have rich content that serves the visitor. Your best solution is to make your Web site a resource center and a billboard—do both. If you're not sure what content to put on your Web site, think about posting articles, books, tip sheets, top ten lists, symptom/solution ideas, links to other resources, etc. However, choosing which content to add to your Web site becomes more obvious once you've gotten the next distinction, which is . . .

2. Specialty vs. Niche.

A specialty is a skill set or unique talent. A niche is the people that you market it to. So, a specialty is about you. A niche describes who buys from you. In the Web, it's important that you come to understand your specialty (what you're really good at) and your niche (who you most want to serve).

3. Domain vs. Web site.

A domain is like having your own ZIP code or vanity license plate, but on the Internet. topten.org is a domain name; ibm.com is a domain name. If you're going to have a real identity on the Internet, you'll need your own domain name. You acquire a domain name (in the United States) from a quasi-governmental agency called InterNIC (http://rs.internic.net/cgi-bin/whois). To actually "order" an available domain name, you have to go through an Internet service provider. A Web site, on the other hand, is the content that you put up on the Web.

4. Web site vs. Home page.

A Web site is like a book; a home page is either a one-page summary or the book's table of contents. If you have a Web page or two about yourself, with your picture, links, résumé/services, etc., what you really have is a home page—sort of a "junior" Web site. When you start adding more pages full of content, information, ordering instructions, etc., it becomes a Web site.

5. Search engines vs. Links.

Search engines (like WebCrawler, Yahoo, HotBot, InfoSeek, AltaVista) are like a library card catalog, only interactive. You tell them what you're looking for, and they find it. When you have a Web address (also called a universal resource locater or URL), you can get yourself listed on any of the search engines by going to that search engine and following the instructions. Or, you can go to sites like www.submit-it.com or www.Webpromote.com to be automatically listed with a number of search engines. So, what's a link? A link is a button on another Web site that puts your URL on their page. Visitors at their site can quickly link to your site. But, of course, you'll need to ask the other Web site to put a link from their site to yours.

6. Internet presence provider (IPP) vs. Internet service provider (ISP).

This distinction is important and easy to understand. An ISP has lots of modems so its customers can call a local number and patch in to the Internet. An IPP doesn't have a way for you to call in via your modem. However, both have full-time, dedicated connections to the Internet. This means that either an ISP or IPP can host your domain name. So, why the heck are there IPPs when it would appear that the ISP can do it all? First, because it's really easy for someone to become an IPP—they just need a single line installed, a decent computer, and some software. An IPP is also a bit more of a consultant and can help you craft your Web site, not just host it. This is really important, because if you've ever called an ISP for Web design advice, they'd probably laugh or refer you to a Web designer and wish you well.

7. GIF vs. JPEG (or JPG).

GIF and JPEG are graphic file formats recognized by Web browsers. Most of the still pictures you see on the Internet are either GIFs or JPEGs. Usually, photographs are best created as JPEG files because you can make the files pretty small, which means that they'll download a lot faster. Logos or special type faces are saved as GIF files. How do you "save" or create a GIF or JPEG file? Most scanner or other graphics software allows you to save your files in either format. If your software can't, there are plenty of freeware or shareware programs available that can convert other graphic formats into GIF or JPEG.

8. FTPing vs. Attaching a file to e-mail.

Okay, so you've created a Web site on your computer, but now you want to get the files over to the computer of your ISP or IPP. First, you could save all of your files on a diskette and mail them to your ISP or IPP. (They won't like this, but they'll probably still let you.) Or, you can e-mail—attaching all your Web site files—to your ISP or IPP Webmaster, who would transfer the files to their proper location. However, most ISPs/IPPs really want you to transfer your files yourself into the special area they've created for you on their computer. To do this, you use "file transfer protocol" (FTP) software to access their computer.

9. CGI vs. Hypertext link.

You know how you can just click highlighted words when you're surfing and go easily from one page or one Web site to the next? This is possible because of something called hypertext links. It moves you from one page to the next, so it's kind of interactive but not really. What if you wanted to create a Web site that lets a visitor take a quiz, or automatically sign up for a free e-mail newsletter subscription, or order a product, or add stuff to your Web site? Now you're getting into the land of CGI programming, formerly the home of geeks and goblins. You can do almost anything with CGI programming, depending on your budget. A good CGI programmer has access to existing CGI scripts that can be adapted to meet your needs, thus saving time and expense. And, there's a new breed of user-friendly CGI programs that work with a database by FileMaker Pro or Oracle.

10. One billion customers vs. 100 customers.

Soon, more than one billion folks will be on the Internet. What makes more sense? Using the Web simply to offer your same old products and services in a new way, or changing your business to serve one billion potential customers? Another way to ask the question is, "How could I reinvent/change my product/service so that it would appeal to one billion customers worldwide?" Big question. You may find yourself substantially changing what you offer or how you deliver it.

THE TOP 10 TEN

Ways to Use the Internet to Make Money

1. Get on the Internet and start surfing.

This will get your creative juices flowing. You can't make money on the Internet until you get on it and get a feel for it. Task: Visit 100 Web sites, including 25 sites of companies involved in your industry or field.

2. Create a Web site of your own on *any* subject.

Is your hobby model trains? Can you create great bumper stickers? Are you an accountant? Do you sell insurance? Whatever you have an interest in or do for a living can have its own Web presence. It's not that expensive and you'll quickly learn what works and doesn't work.

3. Offer something for free.

Web surfers expect to get something for free before they'll pay for something. Create something to give away—a free trial, free advice, free product, free information. Offering a free electronic newsletter (an electronic mailing list) is also effective.

4. Link your Web site to 100 search engines and listing areas so that Web surfers can find you!

No one will likely "find" your Web site directly because they won't even know that it's there. But they can and will find you if you list your Web site with the 25 most popular search engines (which work like a card catalog at the public library) and other custom *listings. Web Promote (www.Webpromote.com) does a great job for about $200, or you can list yourself via Submit-It (www.submit-it.com) for free.*

5. Make your Web site a reference/info/solution center.

Potential customers really appreciate tightly written information to help them in their business or life. If you know something about life insurance, write up what you know and put it at your Web site as a tip sheet. If you know about ball bearings, create the Internet Ball Bearing Museum. So what if others are doing the same thing? It doesn't matter. Start where you can. Within a year, you'll likely find a niche market, see an opening, or find a better way to attract attention and sell your product or service.

6. Come up with an entirely different product or service that will appeal to 100 million people.

One of the cool things about the Web is that the cost of "creating a company" is so small, you can afford to experiment with new products and services. There is always something new to create that will appeal to tons of people at a price they can afford. Think bigger—far beyond your current business. Seek to serve.

7. Become a real entrepreneur and set up 100 Web sites!

This machine gun approach works! It's hard to know exactly what products or services will become most popular and lucrative, so why not offer a variety of items and see what the public wants? Along the way, you'll pick up on a lot of Web skills, too, which always come in handy!

8. Help others get on the Web or offer a Web-related service.

The Web is so new that guides, consultants, and coaches are still needed. You can learn the basics within a month or two and be an "expert" to some degree—at least you'll know ten times more than a "newbie" does! And, during your learning curve, you may come up with a product or service idea that would have made your entry easier and faster—perhaps you can sell that!

9. Sell what sells; don't push what people won't buy.

Get on the Web to become an entrepreneur, not just to push your current product or service via the Web. Let the Web affect you; let the possibilities inspire you; let the low entry cost excite you into creating an entirely different business than the one you currently have. Commerce is moving to the Web quickly, but you may need to start selling different products and services than you do now.

10. Get a Web coach.

Creating a Web site can be really frustrating for the newbie. Get a Web coach who is also a Web presence provider, which is like an Internet service provider (ISP), but offers Web site hosting/consulting services instead of offering dial-in access. So you'll likely have your own ISP and also use a company to host your Web site.

Reasons the Web Is Becoming So Popular

1. It has lots of free stuff.

Offer people free stuff and they'll come.

2. You can find almost anything on it.

Thought the Yellow Pages and the public library were helpful? Hardly. Thanks to improving search engines and screening systems, you can use the Internet to find exactly what you want in minutes.

3. The cost to surf is virtually nil.

Soon, 24-hour-a-day home Web connections will be the norm.

4. The cost to join is virtually nil.

When the entry cost (that is, the cost of putting up a Web site), is nil or low, companies and consumers have fewer reasons not to join.

5. You can access the biggest mall in the world and get what you want at the best price.

Nobody likes to overpay, and the Web will soon offer the most efficient, inexpensive, and even rewarding way to shop and buy. And every consumer becomes an educated consumer, thanks to on-line reviews, technical assistance, comparison shopping, and even public opinion—all available at your fingertips.

6. **People are tired of being couch potatoes, and now are becoming mouse potatoes.**

It's not that big of a leap from TV to the Web; there's a built-in population that has a relationship with a monitor and a remote.

7. **The Web is mesmerizing, stimulating, and evocative.**

You grow from the experience. You think differently. Humans want to be affected, and the Web touches a person in many ways: auditory, visual, emotional, intellectual, spiritual, even tactile and kinesthetic.

8. **The media is hyping it (which is not a bad thing).**

The Web is becoming popular because it's reached critical mass—it's now woven into the fabric of American life. Many folks are getting on-line just not to be left behind!

9. **It's an empowering tool for creativity, entrepreneurism, and communication.**

Any individual can leverage an idea using the Web.

10. **It has created a worldwide social network.**

You feel more a part of the human experience by being connected "with the world." Humans are social beings. The Web is the ultimate community network.

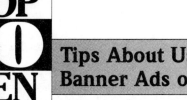

Tips About Using Banner Ads on Web Sites

Banner ads are those clickable pictures at the top of some Web pages. Banner advertising is currently the most popular form of advertising on the Web. There is much debate on its effectiveness and appropriateness, but it's here to stay.

1. Put a blue border around the banner ad.

This reminds the viewer that it's clickable. You can add a blue border within the GIF file itself or use an HTML tag code to do the same thing.

2. Include the words "Click Here" or "Tap Here" somewhere in the banner ad itself.

This increases the click rate significantly.

3. Link the banner ad to a specific page, not just to the home page of a Web site.

Make sure the page the surfer lands at is exactly what's promised in the ad. It helps to have a specific page for each banner ad. Nobody wants to plow through a home page to get to what they want to see.

4. **Create a number of banner ads around a similar theme or look.**

Tout various features of the same product or use different ways to describe the service, but use similar typefaces, colors, and images. This provides continuity and familiarity, yet each ad is different enough to attract attention and make its point.

5. **Change or cycle your banner ads every two weeks.**

The click rate on the same banner ad drops significantly after two weeks.

6. **Add a "click here for offer XYZ" below the ad itself.**

Using standard HTML / text, reinforce the clickability of the banner ad by adding a linked message in small text below the ad / GIF.

7. **Use animated GIFs in the banner ad.**

Motion attracts attention and may lead the surfer to believe that you've got something special. Animated GIFs are becoming standard on Web pages.

8. **Use a deadline/last day/last chance approach in your banner ad.**

This prompts the surfer to take advantage of your special offer right now.

9. **Think of the banner ad as a mini-billboard. It's gotta grab, not just inform.**

Just like a billboard has to grab the attention of a driver whizzing by at 60 miles an hour, your ad needs to grab the Web surfer's attention quickly. Be clever—anything to get them to notice your ad and click on it. Anything!

10. Offer an inducement in your banner ad.

Special contests, prizes, and free offers grab attention. Remember, you are competing for the surfer's attention. No matter how good your product/service/link is, it won't get surfers to tap on your ad unless you pique their curiosity.

Ways to Make Web Sites Interactive

Web sites are becoming highly interactive. To be interactive, a site needs more than just content; it needs some form of a database or other CGI programming. Below is a list of the types of interactivity that are growing more popular. A current list, which is linked to working examples, is located at www.Weboncall.net.

1. Let visitors complete virtual polls and surveys.

Learning about the visitors to your site is key. Asking them questions about themselves and their interests is a good way to get data. But be warned, many visitors today give false information or resent being asked questions, so you'll need to make it an option to respond, not a requirement to get into your site. You can usually get away with requiring such data in return for something free.

2. Give your guests an opportunity to test themselves.

People love to know who they are, what's important to them, and how they compare to others. Whether it's a personality profile, an aptitude tests, a situational quiz, or some other self-awareness test, these are the kinds of things that get people involved in your site.

3. Let visitors add content to your site.

One way to make your site more interactive is to invite your visitors to add information and content to your site, to be viewable by others. The Top Ten site (www.topten.org) does a great job of this; enough Top Ten lists are now being created that the daily top ten list e-mail broadcast can sustain itself forever!

4. Invite guests to leave comments.

Asking for suggestions and feedback about your site, your products, or your services—and then automatically posting these suggestions on your site for all visitors to read—is just smart business today. Why not turn over market research to your potential and current customers? Many are happy to solve problems for you and give you free ideas.

5. Create a community of your customers.

By setting up message boards, chat rooms, and other topic-specific features, you'll be creating virtual communities of visitors with similar interests—and keep them coming back to your Web site. With all those people out there hungering for a sense of community in their lives, these virtual communities are a natural.

6. Offer free newsletters/mailing lists.

Giving visitors something to sign up for turns your site into something interactive! Plus, this way, you can keep coming to them instead of relying on them to come back to you.

7. Create a game.

Did you know that you can now play Scrabble on-line with others? And this is just the beginning—there are hundreds of game sites. Not in the game business yourself? No problem. Just turn part of your book, product, or service into a game that others can play on-line and you'll attract folks.

8. Create an on-line training program with audio and video.

You could combine information with RealAudio (www.realaudio. com) or streaming video and train folks via your Web site. Want to teach someone how to coach better? Audiotape situational examples and then walk the "student" through the process, prompting them for their input and then testing to show the student that they got it (or didn't).

9. Create a flashcard-type training program.

If there is just information you want the person to learn, why not create the info on a series of flashcard-type pages (including text, and/or graphics/sound/video), with links to the right answer and explanations about why the incorrect answers are incorrect.

10. Offer writing aids.

We've created the "Jane Smart Letter," a marketing letter for coaches that the user can customize. So, our template is a great starting-point for the visitor to use. (Go to www.topten. org/janesmart.htm and select "Interactive Web site Examples" to see how the "Jane Smart Letter" works.) The point is that you can be an on-line coach to your visitors in your area of specialty.

THE TOP 10 TEN

Mistakes People Often Make with Their Web Sites

A Web site may be an investment in networking, creating, and learning that pays for itself many times over. These are some of the major reasons that many people don't experience this value.

1. **They put up the Web site, then abandon it.**

Make your Web site a continually expanding resource center. Don't be afraid to give away everything you know.

2. **They make it a second- or third-class Web site.**

It doesn't have to cost much more to make a first-class Web site.

3. **They expect it to be a revenue machine during the first month or year.**

Few enterprises off the Web earn huge profits in their first year. Why should enterprises on the Web be any different?

4. **They assume that people will visit it just because it is there.**

Publish and market the existence of your site.

5. **They try to cut corners by bartering with someone for their Web pages.**

Don't take your Web presence too lightly or be afraid to put money into it. You don't have to spend a fortune, just an amount consistent with your belief in it.

6. **They create an electronic billboard, instead of a Web site.**

Don't just have the visitor see you and how great you are; help them see themselves working with you at your Web site.

7. **They build a surf-by Web site.**

Provide some depth, or something of continuing contact, like a daily, weekly, or monthly newsletter.

8. **They assume that a Web site is all that it will take to bring in business.**

The Web site is just a part of your marketing activities. An e-mail broadcast list and a fax network are equally important. Web sites are passive; e-mail is active. Do both.

9. **They hoard information.**

Don't be stingy. Make your Web site a resource center for the visitor. Give away everything you know. People will bring you new gifts of learning.

10. **They take it too seriously.**

It's okay if it's funny, fascinating, whimsical, or quirky. Don't be afraid to have more than one Web site.

Benefits of Becoming an
IPP/Web Server/Webmaster

Due to reduced costs and availability, hosting your own site has become "the" thing to do for many. The list below contains the reasons I decided to become my own IPP and the benefits that I've received.

1. It's fun.

Hey, the Web is supposed to be fun! Having a 24-hour connection, and playing around with software and cool stuff being developed is a joy. I am not a programmer, techie, engineer, or anything of the sort. I find new things hard to learn. But with the right coach or consultant to smooth out the learning curve and blind spots, I got through the bulk of the process in about 30 days.

2. You'll create more Web sites and profit centers.

Having your Internet connection on 24 hours a day, and knowing how to get a domain name in about an hour from InterNIC, can really get you going! You'll create sites for your business ideas. Hey, what's the risk: $100 for the domain name and some of your time. Why not have ten small businesses on the Web? (I have twelve, and counting. Given the ultra-low costs involved, each is immediately profitable. Hmm . . .)

3. You can and will make money if you want to host others' sites.

Even if you're charging others only $50 a month, 100 clients will bring in $72,000 a year. And your expenses? About $2,500 a year for your dedicated connection plus miscellaneous software. You can just host others' sites, but you'll likely find yourself offering consulting, and if you have any graphic sense, creating sites for others.

4. You'll learn HTML.

HTML is the word processing equivalent of the Web. HTML is not difficult to learn, and many new software programs let you bypass most of the HTML coding. Microsoft FrontPage for Windows and Adobe PageMill for the Macintosh work incredibly well. I used the latter to create more than 25 Web sites. But the benefit here is that you'll start to learn the "communciation" tools of the Web, HTML being the primary one right now. It's like when you learned how to use e-mail, all of a sudden you could do so much more! Same thing when you learn the basics of HTML— you'll get creative!

5. You'll feel good serving others.

Once you learn the basics of Web design and Web site hosting, folks will come to you and ask for your help in getting them up on the Web. We've got a couple more years until most businesses and professionals are up on the Web, so you're not too late at all! And, if you've got coaching or writing skills, you'll be able to help them express themselves and attract business. This will make you feel good and you'll learn more about business, marketing, and creativity along the way.

6. You will feel challenged, intellectually and creatively.

If you want to use your mind more, you'll find it will "wake up" during the learning curve of becoming a Webmaster. You'll think and work harder, you'll figure stuff out, and you'll jump from concepts to implementation. On the creative side, you'll come up with interesting and innovative ways to present information in an attractive and exiting way. This stimulation can be very healthy, especially if you've got some smarts but haven't used them much recently.

7. You'll move closer to the top of the curve.

As you get into being a Webmaster, you'll find yourself getting closer and closer to the source of ideas, catching on earlier to trends in this business, eagerly experimenting with new software and approaches in Web site design and hosting. You'll feel way behind at first, but you'll soon find that you're catching up.

8. You'll get into creating interactive Web sites.

I've had a ball creating a couple of sites that offer interactive stuff, like self-testing, exams, and profiles. I feel that this is the future of the Web and it's fun to create stuff that no one else has thought of yet. I learned a bit of database programming (FileMaker Pro) and learned how to connect it to the Web using a "bridge" called Lasso. Now that I've learned these two programs, I have the tools I need to create almost any interactive site, which happens to be my personal interest. As you work on the Web, you'll come in contact with software and other design tools that you'll get excited about working with.

9. The real benefits of becoming a Webmaster are, at this point, unknown and not measurable.

Even with all the benefits that have made becoming a Webmaster worthwhile, I feel strongly that the real benefits have yet to become known or articulated. It's just a feeling, but a strong one, that there's something more to the whole Web thing. I want to be part of it as a co-creator, not just a passenger.

10. You'll save lots of money.

When you become your own IPP/Webmaster, you'll find that your total monthly cost for a dedicated 28.8K connection will be less than $150 a month. Once you've invested in the hardware costs (less than $5,000) and the consulting to get you past the learning curve ($500–$3,000), your costs are minimal and you can set up Web sites for virtually nothing. Enjoy your journey!

THE TOP 10 TEN

Items Every Small Office Needs

1. **A separate phone line for business calls.**

It's usually less than $40 a month.

2. **A stand-alone fax machine, with its own dedicated phone line.**

This is a lot more convenient than just having a fax in your computer. Figure $400 to $800 for a really good plain paper fax machine.

3. **A desktop or laptop computer.**

You should have a minimum 12 megabytes of RAM, audio/video capabilities, a 1 gigabyte hard drive, an 8X CD-ROM drive, an ergonomic keyboard to save your wrists, a high-quality monitor, and a 28.8/33.6K fax/modem. Plan on spending $2,500 for a solid system these days.

4. **The perfect chair.**

Treat yourself to this.

5. **A scanner with optical character recognition capabilities.**

This is particularly important if you have a Web site. Decent scanners run $350 to $900.

6. A music system.

Music keeps you company.

7. Laser printer.

You'll need a 600 dots per inch printer, not 300 dpi or a bubble/inkjet. Your image matters, and you'll only have to spend around $800.

8. A back-up drive.

Get a removable storage device for backing up your crucial computer files every day. You can get a good one for $200 or less.

9. A battery backup and surge protector.

For $150 to $250 you can get a UPS (uninterruptible power supply) system that gives you 5–15 minutes of juice in case the power goes down. You'll never lose another in-process document because the lights flicker!

10. A desk.

Buy one because it's comfortable and useful, not just because it looks nice.

Software That Every Small Office Needs

1. **Word processing software.**

   Microsoft Word, Corel WordPerfect, ClarisWorks

2. **Spreadsheet software.**

   Microsoft Excel, Lotus 1-2-3, ClarisWorks

3. **Database software or contact management software.**

   Microsoft Access, FileMaker Pro, ClarisWorks, ACT!

4. **Backup software.**

   Retrospect Remote, others

5. **Virus-protection software.**

   Norton Antivirus, Virex, others

6. **Web browser.**

   Netscape Navigator/Communicator, Microsoft Internet Explorer, America On-Line

7. **Graphics software.**

   Adobe Photoshop, Canvas, Illustrator, Painter, QuarkXPress, Aldus PageMaker

8. HTML editor/Site creator.

BBEdit, Adobe PageMill, Microsoft FrontPage, HoTMetaL Pro, Netscape Navigator Gold

9. Finance software.

Quicken, QuickBooks, others

10. Other software.

Eudora (e-mail), Acrobat Reader (pdf files), and others

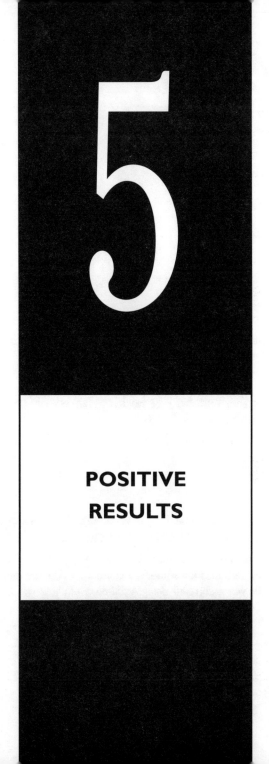

5

POSITIVE RESULTS

Reasons Why Your Future Can Be Great!

In this world of non-linear change, the future can be murky at best. But, if you take a careful look at what's going on in your life, you may find that there's reason for optimism! Read on and see.

1. Your past is over, and you are ready for change.

This is isn't an objective; it's a fact. Your past is over and you can't do anything about it except let go of it. When you do, you are ready for something new.

2. You've recently been hit with issues that you've been avoiding for some time.

This is a signal that it's time—and that you have the capacity—to begin dealing with your life. Issues present themselves for one reason: to be resolved. Contrary to common belief, they do not crop up just to harass you!

3. Your present is filled with challenges, maybe more than you think you can handle.

There's one secret that most successful people discover before they become successful—you can always do more and better than you're currently doing. A full plate of challenges is really an opportunity to discover this for yourself.

4. **Events, people, and problems that "just don't fit" begin to crop up in your life.**

From childhood, we've been tutored by experience to expect things to take a rather linear course, and to anticipate a logical cause-and-effect relationship in most situations. Consequently, it can come as a rude shock to discover that life really isn't that way at all. By trial and experience, we learn the truth of the saying, "A straight line may be the shortest distance between two points, but often it doesn't get you where you want to go!"

5. **You begin to doubt and challenge old beliefs and prejudices.**

This can be discomforting at first. We hold on to our beliefs and prejudices because they serve us well. The problem is that we tend to hold on to them long after they have ceased to serve. When that seed of doubt or challenge begins to creep in, don't resist it; explore it.

6. **Little things begin happening that cause you to feel good or excited.**

When this happens, it marks the beginning of an important discovery: the experience of exhilaration, that sheer joy in being alive. And the important thing about exhilaration is that it can't be forced. Real exhilaration happens.

7. **You become concerned with issues that relate more to others' good than your own.**

Until you've experienced it, no one can tell you how incredibly exhilarating it is to make someone else happy. This "good feeling" is energy—positive, usable power.

8. Words like "service" and "contribution" begin to sound more attractive than words like "profit" and "gain."

If you're in business, profit is important. You won't be in business long without it (unless you have a rich uncle). But profit is just a measure of efficiency, not an assurance of effectiveness. Somewhere beyond increasing profit and sales lies the real reason you're in business in the first place, and it's up to you to figure it out.

9. You feel yourself becoming charged with a sense of accomplishing something significant, even though you're not sure what it is.

Standard management lore has it that we "set" goals and "formulate" visions. Consider for a moment the possibility that visions "emerge" from our consciousness and our subconscious, in a far more complex way than the most sophisticated corporate planning process. The emergence of significance in one's life is a "felt awareness" rather than an intellectual construct.

10. You become willing to commit.

This is one of the big differences between doing what you "should" and what you really want to do. Once you are able to connect with what really turns you on, commitment is almost automatic.

Ways to Be Effective When Working at Home

Most of the suggestions below use external means to keep you working, instead of going down the willpower track, which is fraught with effort!

1. Set deadlines that have negative consequences if you miss them.

Ouch. When you have to get something done, you usually do.

2. Have a buddy, colleague, coach, or staff member who keeps you focused.

Rely on others to help you stay focused and productive.

3. If you don't love what you do, change it so that you do.

If you love your work, you don't need to try to stay focused, because you naturally will be.

4. Develop a routine—or don't.

Some folks work better with a schedule, others don't. Get to know your style and preference.

5. Train your family members what work time means.

If that doesn't work, lock the home office door.

6. Make your home office absolutely perfect.

A great home office will help you stay focused.

7. Keep your beverages and snacks close at hand.

If you leave your home office to go to the refrigerator, you may get distracted by what's going on in the rest of your house.

8. Set daily goals.

Having something definite to accomplish every day can help you accomplish the bigger tasks in smaller bites.

9. Get off to a great start for the day.

Whether it's a walk, time with the paper, or a cup of coffee or tea, have your getting-started routine be something that you genuinely like!

10. Have something interesting to work on for the next day.

The day before, plan something exciting for your first task of the day.

Characteristics of Effective Problem Solvers

Have you ever noticed that some people seem to be natural-born problem solvers? Look closer, and you'll discover that problem solving is more a skill than a gift. Effective problem solvers share ten common characteristics.

1. They have an "attitude."

Effective problem solvers see problems as opportunities, a chance to learn something new, to grow, to succeed where others have failed, or to prove that "it can be done." Underlying these attitudes is a deeply held conviction that, with adequate preparation, the right answer will come.

2. They redefine the problem.

Problem solving is a primary consulting skill. Seasoned consultants know that, very often, the client's initial definition of the problem is incorrect or incomplete. They learn to discount statements such as, "Obviously, the problem is that . . ." and follow their instincts.

3. They have a system.

Perhaps the most common model is the old consulting acronym: DACR/S (Describe, Analyze, Conclude, and Recommend/Solve). Effective problem solvers take the steps in order and apply them literally. For example, in describing the problem (the first step), they avoid making premature judgments or ruling out possibilities. In analyzing the information, they are careful that their own prejudices do not interfere. In developing conclusions, they are aware of the need to test them thoroughly. Finally, most astute problem solvers recognize that there is almost always more than one solution, so they develop several alternatives.

4. They avoid the experience trap.

The world is becoming increasingly non-linear. Things happen in pairs, triads, and groups, and they often don't follow traditional lines from past to present and from cause to effect. In such an environment, past experience must be taken with a grain of salt. Seasoned problem solvers know the pitfalls of relying on what worked in the past as a guide to what will work in the future. They learn to expect the unexpected, the illogical, and the non-linear.

5. They consider every position as though it were their own.

For effective problem solvers, standing in the other person's shoes is more than a cute saying. It's a fundamental way of looking at the problem from every perspective. This ability to shift perspectives quickly and easily is a key characteristic of effective problem solvers.

6. They recognize conflict as a common prerequisite to solution.

When the stakes are high in a problem situation, the parties are often reluctant to show their hands and are cautious about giving away too much. In such instances, managed conflict can be an effective tool for flushing out the real facts of a situation.

7. They listen to their intuition.

Somewhere during the latter stages of the fact-finding (description) process, effective problem solvers experience what can best be called "inklings"—gut-level feelings about the situation. When this happens, they listen, hypothesize, test, and re-test. They realize that, while intuition may be partially innate, they must work to develop it.

8. They invariably go beyond "solving the problem."

On a time scale, just solving the problem at hand brings you to the present, to a point you might call "ground zero." Truly effective problem solvers push further. They go beyond simply solving the problem to discovering the opportunities that often lie concealed within the situation.

9. They seek permanent solutions.

Permanent, as opposed to Band-Aid solutions, have two characteristics: (1) they address all aspects of the problem, and (2) they offer acceptable benefits to all parties involved. Symptomatic problem solving, like bad surgery or dentistry, leaves part of the decay untouched, with the result that, over time, it festers and erupts. A permanent solution is one that keeps a problem from coming back to bite you.

10. They gain agreement and commitment from the parties involved.

It's easy, in the heady rush of finding "the answer" to a problem, to fail to gain agreement and commitment on the part of everyone involved. For effective problem solvers, just "going along" via tacit agreement isn't enough. All parties must concur and be willing to commit to the solution.

Types of Results That Can Be Produced

1. **Financial**

More money is made.

2. **Legacy**

You've left your mark on civilization.

3. **Improvement**

Things have gotten better.

4. **Reduction**

Things have gotten simpler.

5. **Integrity**

Things have gotten stronger.

6. **Expansion**

Things have gotten bigger.

7. **Awareness**

People have gotten smarter.

8. **Energy**

People have been touched.

9. Value

People are left with more.

10. Momentum

People are moving faster.

Ways to Triple Your Effectiveness in a Week

1. Expect twice as much from others as you expect from yourself.

Be shameless. And don't hold your company's productivity back by assuming your team won't or can't do twice as much as you can. Let go of any fear of consequence. Get used to hearing people say no to you.

2. Ask for exactly what you want when you want it, not what you think is reasonable.

Create a same-day culture around you, one in which everyone thinks in terms of immediate response, resolution, and request fulfillment. It really can work. Just raise standards. Share with the team why what you need is so important and enroll them to help you on the spot.

3. Have a list of people to whom you can immediately delegate tasks, problems, and ideas.

Develop a reserve of extra folks, standing by. Hand off new projects/tasks/accountabilities within minutes.

4. Get the information you need immediately.

Don't wait. Don't be put off. When they say "no," consider that "no" to be the beginning of the conversation, not the end. Ask to be put on hold, ask for immediate attention or resolution, ask for an exception. If needed, schedule a call-back time when more information will be available.

5. Cut your normal appointment block time in half.

If you usually schedule thirty-minute meetings, cut them back to fifteen or twenty minutes. You'll create instant productivity on both sides. Simply box yourself in, timewise. More will get done, usually without stress.

6. Respond to problems with three times as many resources as are needed.

The highest levels of productivity occur in "Problem-Free Zones." In order to become more problem-free, invest time and resources into solving the source of problems instead of just Band-Aiding them. Consider problem-solving an investment in your company, not an expense.

7. Stop tolerating what you don't like.

Be selfish. Put up with little. Coach and train others to do it your way. You can accommodate and compromise, but don't lower your standards. Productivity and tolerance don't mix.

8. Keep your word.

Be conservative in your commitments. Enjoying living on the plus side of the performance ledger. Keep the integrity in.

9. Beef up systems.

The ultimate in productivity is when things gets done without your involvement, because you set up a system to make it happen. In other words, automate and systematize so that results occur by themselves, through others or by computer.

10. Decline requests.

Say no or negotiate when saying yes is going to burden you.

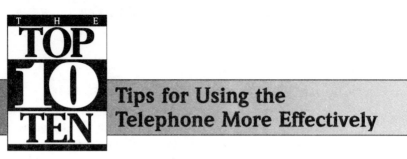

Tips for Using the Telephone More Effectively

The telephone is effective when used efficiently, sparingly, and within the framework of a plan. This list includes some tested guidelines for making the phone a tool that works best for you.

1. Know the purpose of your call.

Most of us talk on the phone too long. Have the purpose of your call clearly in mind before dialing. If helpful, write down a "statement of purpose," together with three main points you want to make on a scratch pad prior to dialing.

2. Know the audience you are calling.

Unless you're conducting "cold calling" for marketing or polling research, you probably know something about your "audience" on the other end. Think of the needs of the person you are calling. Then revise your "statement of purpose" accordingly prior to making the call.

3. Start off right.

State your purpose at the outset, and always ask if it is a good time for the other person to talk. If not, set a specific time to call back.

4. Use names whenever possible.

Identify yourself at the outset of each call. Spell it out, or sound it out, if necessary. Establish the other person's name early in the conversation, and use it often throughout the call!

5. Pay attention and be aware of your tone.

Ask open-ended questions that invite a response. Give the conversation your undivided attention——don't be tempted to do two or three things at once and expect it to be a productive call. Smile! This helps make your voice sound friendly. If you're angry or anxious, put off the call until a later time.

6. Listen carefully.

Pay attention to the first words spoken by the person called. You can learn a lot in the first few seconds by listening carefully. Did you catch the person eating, arguing, gardening, or partying? Decide whether to proceed with the call or to call back, depending upon what you hear in the background of the call. It's better to call back another time than to interrupt—and you'll probably get a better audience!

7. Avoid initiating major business.

Always save the most important business to be conducted in person, if possible. If not, make a careful transition from introduction to the purpose of the call. Remember that a ringing phone virtually always interrupts the party being called—so give them time to adjust before hitting them with something major.

8. Avoid confrontation.

If you have bad news, or a difficult issue to discuss with someone, don't do it by phone unless it's the only way.

9. Be assertive—not aggressive!

Always present your point of view in an assertive, positive way. If you have difficulty being assertive, try making your point while standing during the call. This helps you be more animated and direct, even if the other person can't see you.

10. Conduct a verbal review.

Before concluding the call, go over all agreed-upon points. Repeat necessary dates, times, places and how and when you may be reached.

Ways to Make Sure Your Actions Produce Better Results

1. Identify the exact desired outcome before taking the action.

2. Learn *while* you take action; improve and adjust what you do and how you do it.

3. Take twice as many actions as you think it will take to get the result.

4. Make sure the actions you are taking are the ones that will get the result you want.

5. Make sure you are taking "perfect actions," instead of just being "in action."

6. Make sure that every action you take produces at least *some* measurable result.

7. Be willing to abandon your original objective if something better occurs to you.

8. Make sure the actions you are taking affect others positively and add value to their lives.

9. Make sure you have all the resources you need to follow through when you take action.

10. Make sure that you are the right person to be taking these actions.

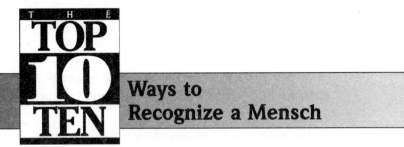

Ways to Recognize a Mensch

A mensch is not just a human being, but a humane being. Without being Pollyannas, these people manage to be positive, optimistic, and generous in their thoughts and deeds towards others. They definitely leave the world better than they found it.

1. They don't interrupt.

2. They take turns.

3. They don't take advantage of people who are feeling down.

4. They are gracious in victory.

5. They are noble in defeat.

6. They are consummately fair.

7. They have integrity.

8. They are the people you want to grow up to be like.

127

9. They are the kind of person you'd want your sister (or brother or daughter or son) to marry.

10. They are the kind of person you'll cherish, if you're lucky enough to have one in your life.

Time Wasters

1. **You allow yourself to be interrupted.**

This may be due to such things as cold calls, unscheduled visitors, or unplanned telephone socializing

2. **You surround yourself with junk.**

Most people have too much junk in the lives—junk e-mail, junk mail, junk meetings, or junk around them. Clear out some of the junk and you'll clear up a lot of your time.

3. **Essential information is poorly organized or non-existent.**

If you can't lay your hands on the essential facts at a moment's notice, you waste time looking for it.

4. **You're burdened with excessive red tape, regulations, and paperwork.**

Delegate what you can't eliminate, but eliminate everything you can.

5. **Policies and procedures are poorly thought-out.**

If your office policies on such things as personnel, correspondence, budget process, expenditures, or crises aren't well conceived and well communicated, you'll waste a lot of time re-inventing them every time an issue arises.

6. Priorities are poorly planned and implemented.

If you and your people don't set sensible priorities, you'll waste time dropping one task in the middle to deal with another that has suddenly become a crisis.

7. You have poor skills in delegating, training, or conceptualizing.

Anything you don't do well impairs your ability to work efficiently. If you lack needed skills, either develop them or delegate the task.

8. You put things off.

If a task has to be done, do it as soon as you can, before it becomes an emergency. If it doesn't have to be done, and you don't want to do it, don't.

9. You don't think through scheduling.

Bad schedules can be worse than no schedules at all. You must allow the right amount of time, at the right time, for everything, keeping in mind other people's schedules when they're working on the same project.

10. You overcommit and then try to do too much at once.

If you're doing too many things at the same time, you're not doing any of them well. Eventually, you'll have to take the time to fix what could have been right the first time.

Steps That Will Help Get You Unstuck

It's not unusual to feel stuck, trapped, and unable to move from a situation you feel is stifling. Actually, it's part of life and growth. But getting "stuck in" and "growing through" situations are different. Here are ten ways to shift from one to the other.

1. Step back and ask yourself what's really going on.

When you're caught up in the stuff of everyday life, it's easy to lose objectivity. It's good to set aside a little time each day to challenge the obviousness of what seems to be going on. Is there a lesson to be learned that you are missing? Might that setback really be a step forward? Will things really turn out as badly as you think they will?

2. Consider whether what's happening has happened before.

Is this a unique situation or is it just another example, in different garb, of an issue you've failed to confront before? If it's the latter, maybe now's the time to solve it and move on.

3. **Assume that present events and circumstances may be less of a "problem" than parts of a larger "process."**

There's a fair case to be made for the notion that, in this life, all is process rather than result. In other words, what this life is really about is growth and learning. Viewed in this light, where you're heading is not as important as how you choose to get there. (For those who are strongly goal-oriented, this may be tough to swallow.)

4. **Ask yourself what you can do next.**

It's the small steps that lead to successful journeys. Don't get sucked in by the suggestion that you've got to solve it all today.

5. **Do something—anything!**

When you're stuck, taking any step puts you in a different place and helps change your perspective, even if it's a wrong move! And, doing something could be a conscious decision to do absolutely nothing! Sometimes, we have to stop "doing" in order to get clear.

6. **Look for support nearby.**

Almost always, help is at hand, a phone call or a touch away. We tend to look way out there or off into the future, thinking that the help we need is just not available to us in our present situation. If, instead, you begin with the assumption that the tools you need to solve the problem are close at hand, you'll be amazed at how it sharpens your vision!

7. **Take the negatives, one by one, and toss them out.**

Negatives can be just as powerful as positives, depending on how much energy you give them. It's your choice.

8. **Take one positive, unselfish project and make it yours.**

Help someone else, even if you think that you're the one who needs help. And don't be surprised if, in your darkest moment, someone comes knocking at your door—asking for help.

9. **If lack is a problem, try substituting the word "service" for profit or gain.**

You "get" from what you lack, but you "give" from what you are. When you begin to consider seriously how you can be of service, it can be absolutely amazing how much you discover you have to give.

10. **Be grateful for every blessing.**

It's not big jumps that lead to greatness—it's small steps. The "little" good things that happen to us (and sometimes they seem to be very little) are tests of our awareness. It pays off not to flunk these tests!

Ways to Use a Virtual Assistant

A virtual assistant is just like an executive assistant or personal assistant, except that the virtual assistant handles your affairs from a distance—and does it electronically. This list reviews the ten most common ways to use the services of a virtual assistant. I've included my own experience below, when appropriate.

1. Pay your bills.

I haven't paid a bill for two years. My virtual assistant, Irene, does all of that for me, using personal finance software, via her computer. All of my bills come to a post office box close to her home. She sends my bank statement to me every month, which is one way I have to verify my bank balance. Of course, embezzlement is a risk, so don't turn over your checking account to someone you don't know well.

2. Screen and forward your mail.

My virtual assistant is sharp; she knows what I want to see and what I don't want to see. I get a weekly envelope from her with just the important stuff. What a relief!

3. Solve problems that you don't want to solve.

I have a virtual assistant on contract whom I pay $100 for every problem I don't want to deal with. I just tell my VA what outcome I want, answer her questions, and wait for the e-mail confirming

---

that it's done. Now, this isn't always perfect, but it works most of the time. Just knowing that I have someone to delegate problems to is a great feeling!

4. Screen and handle e-mail.

Virtual assistants can review all of your e-mail, handle what they can, and pass on the rest for you to handle. This can free up an hour or two a day and is reason enough to have a VA. Your VA just goes into your incoming e-mail queue several times a day. For confidential matters, you can set up a private e-mail address that you only give to select people.

5. Manage projects or reporting.

My VA has a weekly checklist of the information, statistics, or reports I need for a number of my projects. Sure, I could compile them myself, but why? I'd much rather the VA do it and follow up with the folks who haven't reported in (I'm not a good "chaser"). Sure, it's cheating, but what's wrong with living an insulated life?

6. Follow up with clients or other contacts.

I'll e-mail my VA to follow up with a client who missed a call, or to ask a colleague how I can help them do something that I know they are working on, or to schedule a time to chat with a colleague. Do the colleagues mind that I've delegated this to my VA? Yes, they are offended sometimes, but only until they get their own VA.

7. Remind you of important dates.

Your VA can handle all of your scheduling and even remind you of anniversaries, birthdays, or reporting dates.

8. Point out what you cannot see.

*My VA sometimes says, "Hey, Thomas, did you know that . . ."
I love this! It lets me focus on what I want to focus on instead
of having to keep my eye on everything.*

9. Screens and handles your phone messages.

*Your VA can tap into your voice mail several times a day and
clean it out, leaving you the calls that you need to handle.
Again, your VA is more than your assistant and more than a
message taker or message deliver. Your VA is you and acts on
your behalf, protecting you and your time from the demands
of others. You'll need to train your VA on how to be you, but this
will pay off handsomely. I empower my VA to set policy, make
exceptions, solve problems, make mistakes, coordinate efforts,
screen heavily, anticipate my needs and be a partner.*

10. Develop systems of support.

*I don't just ask my VA to do stuff or handle tasks, but also to
create systems so that things of a similar nature get handled
automatically in the future. Most VAs need support and training
on how to do this, but once they get it, you're all set for a
problem-free and task-free environment.*

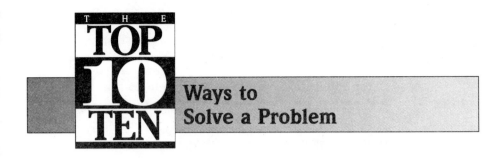

1. Ignore it for a while; see if it solves itself.

2. Declare it to be a crisis and invest many resources to solve it.

3. Give the problem to someone whose job it is to solve it.

4. Identify the source of the problem first.

5. Throw money at it.

6. Accept that it's *not* a problem at all and treat it like the opportunity that it is!

7. Do the opposite of what you'd normally do to solve the problem.

8. Identify the five steps that will solve the problem.

9. Extend your boundaries immediately so that this type of problem doesn't happen again.

10. Change yourself, or increase your perspective, so that it's no longer a problem.

Things to Do When You Feel Blocked

Feeling stuck and unproductive is natural and it can be caused by overwork, lack of momentum, a bad mood, a success block, the weather, or dozens of other factors. While it can be helpful to understand why you're stuck and unproductive, sometimes it's just better to do one or more of the *practical* things that follow!

1. Play the check-in game.

Call a friend and say, "I'm stuck. Can I check in with you every hour for a couple of hours until I get cranking again?" This really works! Your friend may want to play along, too! Just share what you want to get done, specifically, between now and the next time you call in. Your friend can either listen and accept what you're saying—or ask you to increase or decrease the goal for the hour. In either case, keep the check-in call under five minutes.

2. Take a walk, go to the gym, go running, or move your body.

Increasing your body's metabolism also loosens up your mind and spirit, resulting in a greater energy flow. It's that simple.

3. Take a nap.

Sometimes, your mind needs a break to work through an idea or block. Take a short nap and see if that helps.

4. Turn up the music.

I use music as a prompter, especially when I'm feeling draggy or alone. Rap, disco, and instrumentals work for me. And when I'm really stuck, Frank Sinatra does the trick.

5. Eat or drink something that you will respond to emotionally or physically.

If I'm really stuck, I'll have a couple of cups of coffee. Caffeine is a great unblocker for me.

6. Completely clean up your workspace.

Disorganized "stuff" around you can be a energy drain. When I get stuck, one of the first things I do is take a few minutes and put things in piles, file stuff away, or clear my immediate work area so that there's less stuff dragging me down.

7. Work on another task or project.

I don't know about you, but I'm not willing to push myself through a project that I'm just not in the mood to work on. So, I find a project that I do want to work on and my productivity picks right up!

8. Have a routine.

A routine provides momentum, and momentum will keep you from getting stuck. So, schedule in an hour or so of dedicated work between appointments.

9. Play the reward game.

This may not be spiritually healthy, but I reward myself when I finish a tough project. It may be a vacation, a trip, a shirt, a massage, or anything that works for you.

10. Go on a trip.

I find that I'm especially creative when on a plane, train, or bus. So, sometimes, I'll book a short hour trip, bring my laptop, and be incredibly productive. It's worth it!

Things to Do When You Have Five Minutes or Less

This list is meant simply to be suggestive of things to do when you are waiting for a client, standing in line, waiting to be seen by the next available clerk, or sitting on hold. See how many other things you can think of to do in under five minutes!

1. Read your mail.

Carry an envelope or two in a store with you. When you have to wait in line, take it out to read.

2. Check your weekly appointment schedule.

A daily calendar is a great companion in a line or waiting room. Use the time to keep it current.

3. Write a note or dictate a memo into a portable cassette recorder.

No time to write? Why not dictate a note for your assistant to type up and send later? Even a few minutes in a line will provide the time needed to outline a letter.

4. See who is within a few feet of you to chat with.

It's amazing how effective networking can be when we're willing to smile and strike up a conversation with others waiting nearby. "It sure is a hot (cold) day" can turn into a tremendous friendship or business adventure if we dare to share.

5. Outline your thoughts on paper.

Have a speech to give? a paper or report to write? Use these few minutes to organize and be clear about your intentions.

6. Make a quick phone call.

A cellular phone is terrific to use while waiting in lines—but a nearby pay phone will do, too. Take a few minutes to order something nice to be delivered to your spouse. Call the client you've been putting off getting back to, and make it clear that your time is quite limited.

7. Practice deep breathing or relaxation exercises.

You may seem a bit strange to others—but you'll definitely feel better for it.

8. Read something close by that you would not otherwise take time to examine.

The magazine section at the supermarket check-out line is a good example. Now is the time to examine some publication you would probably never buy for yourself.

9. Clear away your clutter.

This is a terrific time to go through your pockets, calendar, attaché case, or purse and get rid of the old gum wrappers, envelopes, and miscellaneous papers. Lighten up.

10. Floss your teeth.

You may want some privacy in a nearby rest room or hallway for this one—but why not? It's a good habit, and your dentist and teeth will thank you for it.

Electronic Tools for Increasing Your Productivity

1. Voice mail

2. Computer

3. Copier/scanner/printer/fax machine

4. Text pager

5. Microcassette recorder

6. Cellular phone

7. Fax modem

8. Credit/debit card

9. PDA (like a Newton)

10. E-mail

Ways to Reach a Goal Faster

1. Install a consequence that really, really hurts!

2. Hire a short-term coach who will help you make it happen.

3. Break the goal down into important pieces and enjoy the momentum as you accomplish each one.

4. Link the goal to one of your values so that it becomes an expression of yourself rather than this "thing" that you're working on.

5. Know the next goal you want to accomplish, even before you have fully started on the immediate goal. This creates perspective and context, making the current goal look much easier!

6. Find a way to be rewarded as you go. A runner sips water continually—she doesn't gulp it down at the end.

7. Start feeling and acting as if the goal has already been reached and then just do what it takes to "finish" it.

8. Eliminate the consequences of nonperformance and just work on taking daily actions instead—get your juice from taking action rather than measuring up to the goal.

9. Set an earlier end point and orient everything around reaching the goal by then.

10. Change the goal so that it *can* be reached easily. Who says you should pick only the tough goals?!

Ways to Slow the Flow of Attraction

Attraction is the idea that we all draw things, people, opportunities, and even our "higher selves" to us. The trick is to attract the best of these, not everything. Along that line, here are some of the things to do that will limit or slow down your natural attractive powers.

1. Lie to yourself or others.

Not telling the truth, kidding yourself, living a pipe dream, exaggerating, and pretense all undermine your integrity.

2. Overload your life.

Cramming your life so full of things prevents anything new from flowing in.

3. Accumulate what's not needed.

Avoid seeking to grab whatever you can, whenever you can.

4. Mislabel.

Don't mistake your ego for yourself. Sometimes the line is confusing.

5. Assign too much significance to people, things, or events.

Don't make things more important or significant than they really are.

6. Become dependent or attached.

Resist becoming attached to a person, situation, goal, substance, belief, idea, or job to the point where you live for it or them instead of relating with life itself.

7. Ignore what life is bringing you.

Focus on what life is bringing you, not just what you think you should be focusing on.

8. Acquire attractiveness.

Be yourself, don't try to emulate what you think is attractive about others.

9. Be needy.

Find your answers within yourself; don't expect others to provide you with self-satisfaction.

10. Don't trust yourself.

Honor your inklings, instincts, and intuitions.

Causes of Job Burnout

1. **You find you're suffering on the job.**

Maintain the distinction between pain and suffering. Pain is inevitable; suffering is optional. Don't suffer.

2. **You feel pushed to produce beyond your limits.**

Work on saying no.

3. **You promise too much and then barely keep up.**

Are you addicted to adrenaline?

4. **You give too much and don't get enough back.**

Are you underappreciated? Consider lowering your expectations or moving elsewhere.

5. **The people at work drain you.**

Again, examine your boundaries. Do you let people take advantage of you?

6. **You don't get ahead the way you want.**

What are your expectations? Are they reasonable? Establish a plan for achieving your goals.

7. You've lost interest in what you used to enjoy doing.

Routine bores everyone eventually. Find ways to expand your scope at work. Take on new projects.

8. You've developed feelings of depression.

Take care of your mental health. It will affect everything you do. It's okay to get professional help.

9. You're feeling angry and withholding communications.

Who are you trying to punish? Why?

10. You're having personal problems unrelated to the job.

A happy person is a productive employee; an unhappy person is an unproductive employee.

6

INSPIRED
MANAGEMENT

Factors That Contribute to Problem Behavior

Most employees perform acceptably, if not exceptionally, under sometimes trying conditions. Occasionally, however, it's the problem behaviors of a few that consume much of the manager's time. Here are ten factors that can contribute to problem behavior in the workplace.

1. Employees have been given inadequate standards, poor training, or too much responsibility too soon.

Employees take their cue from you, their boss. If you haven't set clear standards, or haven't seen to it that your employees have the training needed to do their jobs, the results will show up in sloppy work habits, lagging productivity, poor quality work, and confusion.

2. The company has set conflicting objectives.

Congruity, or at least correspondence, between individual and organizational objectives is imperative to a smoothly managed operation. It is the manager's responsibility to help establish the connections between these two sometimes opposite poles. If employees do not perceive that they have an identifiable stake in the enterprise, their enthusiasm and effort will wane and their tacit or overt resistance will rise.

3. The boss is arrogant.

A CEO friend remarked that "being a successful CEO in today's world requires a certain amount of controlled arrogance." I disagree. Ego, arrogance, and disparities between word and action are antagonistic to effective leadership. Further, they are triggers likely to set off rounds of employee resentment.

4. The company tolerates poor performance.

Laziness and lack of motivation on the part of boss or employees lead to average performance at best and, at worst, behaviors that soon get out of control, such as foot-dragging, grousing, and blaming. Strong motivation and exceptional performance come from high self-esteem. It is the manager's responsibility to make positive demands on employees that they may surpass even their own notions of how capable they are.

5. The boss shares his or her weaknesses with employees.

Some managers attempt to build rapport by sharing their problems, fears, and shortcomings with their employees. Predictably, the results of these efforts are usually opposite from those anticipated. Employees resent the thought that the boss is less than an accomplished professional.

6. The boss is intolerant of failure.

Bosses who accept only successes from their employees create an environment where caution rather than risk prevails. Failure, in many cases, is simply the price that must be paid for learning and for subsequent higher performance. To some extent, the boss is coaching, encouraging, cajoling, challenging, and applauding even the failures when they lead to greater awareness of what it takes to succeed.

7. The company or its officers practice dishonesty.

The recent emergence of "ethics managers" in some organizations suggests that ethical behavior and honesty have not been adequately recognized as contributing to long-term corporate success. One such officer—revealing what might have been the starting point for his assignment, spoke candidly of the need to develop a policy with respect to the "ethics of compromise." Employees don't see it that way. While the issue may be gray when viewed from the executive suite, for those at the working level, it is clearly black and white.

8. There is a lack of discipline by example.

In this age of flat organizations, cross-functional teams, and multiple reporting relationships, discipline is instilled more by example than by fiat. The boss who arrives late and leaves early, or accepts less than excellent work from himself or others, has no cause to complain when the work of the unit is below par. Exemplary performance on the part of the boss—being able to say confidently, "do as I do and as I say"—leads to higher productivity, greater cohesiveness, and reduced problems on the job.

9. Managers lead by instruction rather than discovery.

If you, as a manager, aren't aware of the difference between these two, and are not willing to forgo the first in favor of the second, you can anticipate problems with your employees. One role of the manager is to teach, but in today's workplace, where informed workers reign, teaching must be attended by a subtle awareness of what it takes to stimulate, intrigue, and learn, especially in complex task areas.

10. Companies "step over" problems instead of dealing with them.

Bosses who procrastinate in dealing with employee problems can expect to see them multiply and expand. The rule is—and there are few exceptions—"step over it today and you'll fall over it tomorrow."

Secrets of Effective Delegating

1. **Delegate to someone who is naturally responsible and accountable.**

If you expect (or tolerate) anything less, you've got a problem.

2. **Link performance to salary.**

Make the successful completion of the task or accountability that you're delegating a requirement for getting paid.

3. **Identify what the signs and measures of failure are.**

This way, you can inform the person, in advance, what isn't acceptable, and what you'll be "looking out for."

4. **Identify the measurables of the job.**

Then, you'll both know if the job is getting done.

5. **Develop an iron-clad reporting system.**

This could be a daily checklist, a weekly report, a monthly financial statement, or a weekly meeting. Whatever it takes.

6. **Create an oversight process.**

Have someone you trust check up on the employee's performance, results, accuracy, and honesty.

7. Identify the consequences for inadequate performance, in advance.

If you do this, there are no surprises, and whatever actions you take are not punitive or arbitrary.

8. Double-check the work yourself from time to time.

This means review the work, chat with customers, and get outside verification.

9. Build in a system of continuous improvement of the delegated task or accountability.

This keeps the employee focused on creating new and better ways of doing what you need.

10. Customize an incentive package, if appropriate.

All employees have their own ways of becoming motivated. Make sure that you understand them and create something around that, not around your own way. But don't be too generous—that usually backfires. Remember, you're their employer, not their friend or business partner.

Benefits to Offer Employees

1. Give them a competitive salary and regular raises.

2. Establish performance-based bonuses.

3. Provide equity ownership via employee stock ownership plans or partnership.

4. Supply them with the latest, coolest tools and equipment to do their job well.

5. Provide recognition, attribution, credit, acknowledgment, and visibility.

6. Grant them power, authority, responsibility, a voice, and a place on a team.

7. Offer perks such as cars, discounts, expense accounts, or a larger office.

8. Give them time off for vacation, rest, and regenerating.

9. Make sure they have plenty of ongoing training, schooling, and education, both personal and professional.

10. Come up with custom items like Thinking, Reeingineering, or Clean-up Days.

Ways to Empower Others

1. Find out what they most want in life right now and package what you are selling to meet that need.

Stand next to people and "look" with them at their future and their lives, and discuss what both of you see for them.

2. Ask a question that gets them to think bigger and to expect more out of life and themselves.

People love to be expected to want more for themselves. You become Santa Claus!

3. Find out what's blocking them from buying and address it directly until *they've* resolved it.

Get them to tell the truth; if they can't see it and express it, express the resistance for them so they can be relieved of it. When someone can properly express their true objection, they can let it go more quickly.

4. Be an example of how the product or service really works.

Walk it, don't just talk it. Believe so much in what you're selling that it's contagious.

5. **Be someone special enough that those you speak to want to become more like you.**

People often buy something because there was a quality about the salesperson that they admired enough that they wanted to adopt it.

6. **Understand that most people need to be asked seven times to buy something.**

Assume that the first six no's are simply requests for more information or a better reason to buy. Not everyone is as quick to choose as most salespeople are. Some folks want to be sold; they expect it. Don't be bashful. Be proud of what you sell.

7. **Get permission to ask tough questions.**

This is respectful, builds trust, and also gets them saying the word "Yes," which is always a good start!

8. **Don't be fazed by anything the person is saying.**

If you've decided that what you're selling is good for them (like really good for them), help them to see this and why. This will keep you from getting scared or stopped by whatever they say as they are resisting.

9. **Even when they've said yes, listen for the no's and address those.**

You want the yes to stay a yes, forever. Any unresolved no's have a way of growing and choking the yes within a day or a month.

10. **Believe in them.**

When someone believes in you, you'll tend to accept them and buy!

Tips for Handling Employee Problem Behavior

If you've been a manager for long, you know that things can go wrong even in the best of organizations. Problem behavior on the part of employees can erupt for a variety of reasons. Here are ten tips for dealing with it.

1. Recognize that employee problem behavior usually has a history.

It usually develops over time and seldom from a single incident. As a manager, it is your responsibility to be alert to the early warning signs and deal with the underlying causes before the situation reaches a crisis level.

2. Ask yourself: "Am I partly or wholly responsible?"

You would be surprised how frequently a manager has created, or at least contributed to, problems of employee behavior. An abrasive style, being unwilling to listen, and being inattentive to the nuances of employee behavior are factors that contribute to the manager's ability to thoroughly examine what is going on.

3. Don't focus only on the overt behavior.

When confronted by an angry employee, it's easy to attack the person and target the behavior rather than examine the factors that underlie the behavior. Often, this takes patience, careful probing, and a willingness to forgo judgment until you really understand the situation.

4. Be attentive to the "awkward silence" and to what may be missing.

When an employee is reluctant to communicate, it's an almost sure sign that more lurks beneath the surface. Often, employees will withhold because they feel unsafe. They may test the waters by airing a less severe or kindred issue in order to see what kind of a response they get. It's imperative that the manager read between the lines and offer the concern and support necessary to get the employee to open up.

5. Clarify before you confront.

Chances are, when an issue surfaces, you will be given only a fragmentary and partial picture of the problem. You may have to dig deep to discover important facts, and talk to others who may be involved. One safe assumption is that each person will tend to present the case from his or her viewpoint, which may or may not be the way it really is.

6. Be willing to explore the possibility that you have contributed to the problem.

This isn't easy, even if you have reason to believe it's so, because you may not be fully aware of what you have done to fuel the fire. Three helpful questions to ask yourself are (1) "Is this problem unique, or does it have a familiar ring to it?" (2)"Are others in my organization exhibiting similar behaviors?" and (3) "Am I partially the cause of the behavior I am criticizing in others?"

7. Plan your strategy.

Start by defining what changes you would like to see take place. Then follow this sequence: (1) State the problem to the employee as you understand it and explain why it is important that it be resolved; (2) Gain agreement that you've defined the problem correctly; (3) Ask for solutions, using open-ended questions such as: "What are you willing to do to correct this problem?" In some cases, you may have to make it clear what you expect; (4) Get a commitment that the employee will take the required actions; (5) Set deadlines for completing the actions. In the case of a repeated problem, you may want to advise the employee of the consequences of failing to take corrective action; (6) Follow up on the deadlines you've set.

8. Treat the employee as an adult and expect adult behavior.

To some extent, expectations define the result. If you indicate, by your actions or by the tone of your voice, that you expect less than full adult behavior, that's what you're likely to get.

9. Treat interpersonal conflicts differently.

If the problem behavior stems from a personality conflict between two employees, have each one answer these questions: (1) How would you describe the other person? (2) How does he or she make you feel? (3) Why do you feel that the other person behaves the way he or she does? (4) What could you do to alleviate the situation? (5) What would you like the other person to do in return?

10. Seek agreement regarding steps to be taken and results expected.

Nothing is really "fixed" unless it stays fixed. All parties to a dispute must agree that the steps taken (or proposed) will alleviate the problem substantially. Furthermore, they must agree on what they will do if the problem isn't fixed.

Secrets of Effective Team Interaction

Teams have been touted as a way to replace managers, evoke initiative, assist in leadership development, and save the Queen. In reality, the synergy that's possible in teamwork usually turns out to be chaos. Here are ten tips on making the most of your team.

1. Give the team (or have them create) a big enough vision or outcome.

If the goal isn't bigger than the personalities of the team members, the team's effectiveness will be mediocre.

2. Train all team members in the standards of behavior for communication, response, and interaction.

These ground rules are designed to keep the team's communication clear and make team membership mean something. Bad attitudes, delayed responses, nattering, gossiping, whining, or politicking are grounds for expulsion.

3. Have the team elect the team leader.

Leadership is still required in a team environment. Not a manager, but a team leader. A team leader should have the confidence of everyone, and not be the person with the power to hire and fire, unless the members are okay with that.

4. Install structures to support the team and keep it moving.

Daily or weekly reporting, and public display of team goals and results help everyone on the team understand that they are on a team and that the team is accomplishing something.

5. Teams need a member who manages the details and flow of ideas and information.

Have one team member be the person who makes sure that ideas are catalogued, agreements are kept, promises are made, and input from team members accomplishes good things instead of disappearing into the ether.

6. Hold periodic meetings in which the *only* agenda is how the team can work together better.

It's imperative that two things happen, otherwise these "effectiveness" meetings become just gripe sessions. First, make it a ground rule that any unresolved issues among team members must be resolved prior to the next effectiveness meeting. Second, have every team member make one suggestion for team effectiveness prior to the meeting, so they can propose it during the meeting.

7. Know when a team approach is called for and know when it's "not enough."

8. Provide continual, accurate, and frequent acknowledgment.

A big part of what makes the synergy of a team work is that team members are publicly acknowledged for what they've done to help the team and its goal. However, keep this praise accurate rather than just manipulative puffery.

9. Team meetings should be exciting moments of creating, not reporting.

Pose a great question or significant problem for the meeting; don't make it a boring reporting session. That's why we have e-mail and copy machines. If there's any reporting to do, keep it short and positive.

10. Teams work best when people enjoy each other's company.

Use the team meetings and team approach to deepen relationships, from which effectiveness and profitability naturally increase.

THE

TOP 10 TEN

Employee Audit Questions

1. How do we measure productivity?

2. How do we measure quality of production?

3. How do we create loyalty?

4. How well do we hire and how do we know?

5. Do our employees know who their customers are and who they are a customer of, internally?

6. How well rewarded are our employees?

7. How happy are our employees?

8. Do our employees know the advancement track here, and do we help them succeed?

9. Where are we not acknowledging our employees adequately?

10. Which key employees are thinking about leaving?

Ways to Retain Good Employees

Retaining good employees has always been a challenge. This is true even more so today in light of the widespread suspicion and cynicism of management that downsizing causes. Here are ten things you can do:

1. Share the results of good work tangibly.

Bonuses, cash, and non-cash rewards need to be tied to results so that employees know that they are being rewarded for their specific contribution. Gifts given at the whim of the CEO can be regarded as actually demeaning, in that they bear little relationship to actual contribution.

2. Let your employees know they are part of a team.

Employees have heard the cliché that "people are our biggest asset" so much that they nearly vomit when it is repeated. Letting them know that it's true means having direct, regular, and personal contact. I recall walking around the plant with Jim Lincoln, president of Lincoln Electric, many years ago. Every single one of the 604 employees knew and addressed their president by his first name, and he reciprocated!

3. Follow the CFH rule: Be candid, frank, and honest.

Somehow, the higher one gets on the executive ladder, the more the misconception seems to exist that you can get away with not telling the truth to your employees. That simply isn't so. Being less than honest means that you'll get less than the best from your people.

4. Don't spare the bad news.

Some CEOs have a penchant for spreading the good news and hoarding the bad on the grounds that their employees won't be able to take it. The surprising thing is that, given a chance, most people are more resilient than we think.

5. Little things mean a lot.

Have you ever received a card or note that really lifted your spirits, because someone knew you were down and took the time to let you know that he cared? Taking time to find out what's going on with your employees (yes, after 5:00) and letting them know you care—with a card, a call, or simply a word— can make a huge difference.

6. Recognize that suspicion is normal.

As a manager, you may not want to hear it, but one of the unfortunate effects of downsized America is that CEOs are, in general, not regarded as believable! So, it takes patience, fortitude, and a good deal of practice to get to the point where you are believed by your people. Don't become dismayed. Just keep at it, as long as what you do and say is real.

7. Distribute choice perks.

As long as you are in business to make a profit, your business can't afford to operate as though all people and positions are equal, because they're not! Some people are more talented than others; some have more energy, drive, and concern; and some demand more because they deserve it. For those in this latter category, the true high achievers, you will have to treat them better or lose them. They don't need your guidance as much as your recognition that they are outstanding.

8. Set your boundaries and make them clear.

Every person who reports to you should be absolutely clear about two things: (1) What you expect of them, and (2) what they can expect of you. It pays to have a formal, written boundaries statement to discuss personally with everyone who reports to you.

9. Make it clear that continued growth is a condition of continued employment.

Too many organizations, especially in government, tolerate mediocrity. In the long run everyone, including the employee, suffers. From here into the twenty-first century, there will be less and less room for those who do just enough to get by.

10. Be genuine and be a model.

You would think that this is obvious. Unfortunately, it's not. I've seen so many executives and CEOs who follow the dictum of "Do as I say, not as I do." One of the surprising results of chronic reengineering has been that those employees who are truly self-directing have become less willing to tolerate unacceptable conditions. The average performers will hang around, but the outstanding ones will bide their time and leave.

**Ways to
Leadership, *Now***

This list presents "The New Leadership": How to think like and act like—and even become— a leader, within 24 hours.

1. **Accept that *everyone* can be a leader.**

This is a good thing.

2. **Realize that your opinion is as valid or more valid than another's.**

Develop, expand, and fine-tune your opinions.

3. **Understand that leadership is not about getting people to follow you. It's about moving forward yourself.**

4. **Get in touch with a vision that touches you personally.**

Now you have something worth leading about.

5. **Tell people what you want them to do.**

Challenge them to act or change. This is part of being a leader.

6. Learn from the people you are leading, *and* from those whom you aren't.

Learn from everyone.

7. Become highly sensitized and intuitive.

These are learned skills that keep you ahead of the pack.

8. Become an early-adopter of trends, products, services.

Don't chase every new thing on the block, but do take lots of risks by experimenting.

9. Give value to others and they'll grant you leadership rights.

Humans are selfish—give them what they need and want and they'll let you lead them.

10. Don't try to become a leader.

Just do what you most want to do in your life and business and notice who follows you.

Traps to Avoid When Leading an Organization

1. **Get caught up with the naysayers, small thinkers, small people, and problem-oriented folks.**

Protect yourself. It's just their style of relating. It doesn't need to become yours. Yes, listen to them, but don't get caught up in their dynamic.

2. **Try to serve the customers and staff *en masse.***

Serve the individual and you'll serve the group. Think about Joe Smith, a favorite customer. What can you do to make his business better today?

3. **Put "workability" ahead of your own standards and boundaries.**

You come first. Getting the job done is essential in an organization, but don't compromise or overly rely on "workarounds." Have others do it your way.

4. **Respond to current problems instead of continually investing in the infrastructure.**

Use the current problems you face as the impetus to install better systems. Don't just be a fireman; be a building inspector and architect.

5. Put your boundaries ahead of your standards.

Don't define yourself by what you won't permit. Instead, make yourself a bigger person and have a larger vision. If you do this, you'll find that you don't need to protect yourself from others because folks will "get it" and help to build you up!

6. Sublimate your goals, dreams, and desires for the organization, to what others want.

Trust yourself. Your judgment, opinion, ideas, intuition, and inklings are crucial. Don't get talked into stuff by others. Give yourself more credit, always.

7. Let power-hungry types compete with you.

Either they're on the team or they're outta here. These types are everywhere, often when you least expect them. Either redirect their energy to serve, or ease them out.

8. Compare yourself to the competition, whether they are stronger or weaker than you.

The buggy-whip manufacturers did this and missed a top innovation of the twentieth century: the automobile. Instead of comparing yourself to the competition, seek to better understand the customer you sell to and serve. If you'll just listen, they'll tell you when they want something better or even radically different than you are offering.

9. Assume that current revenue streams will continue beyond a year.

Don't get too comfy. Assume your best profit sources will disappear within 12 months and you'll keep creating the next level!

10. You let the costs inch up or get away from you.

Cut, cut, cut each quarter, even if it hurts. Prune. Don't approve recurring expenses unless there is no other way. Usually it's better to invest capital in equipment and systems to keep costs down.

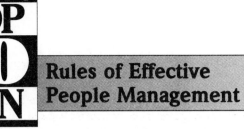

Rules of Effective People Management

$\mathbf{T}$he ten items below (and there are surely more) are a good yardstick to determine your profit potential through people management.

1. Create expectations.

Tell people up front what is expected of them.

2. Set a stretch challenge.

Make people grow, and coach them along the way.

3. Never move too slowly on critical personnel decisions.

Dragging your feet here will really hurt your business.

4. Involve people in both developing and implementing strategy.

Too much top-down brings the top down.

5. Call a spade a spade.

Address poor performance or it'll cost you—big.

6. Reward your stars.

Pay good performers what they're worth, and it will be returned to you tenfold.

7. Get the right person for the job.

Define the job and find the person who can do it rather than redefining the job to fit the capabilities of the incumbent.

8. Require that people do their homework.

When people are not prepared for meetings, the company is not prepared to make decisions. Stop the presses!

9. Constantly upgrade skills.

Provide continuous training to keep people at their best.

10. Recognize that pride drives performance more than money.

Compliment people for a job well done.

Ways to Improve Your Company

1. **Know your personal values.**

What's most important to you personally? When you know your values, you'll better filter new information and opportunities and can rely better on your intuition.

2. **Get candid input from at least five other people who know you well.**

While it's nice to get input from experts, it's as valuable to get points of view from colleagues, family members, and key employees who know you. They know your tendencies and your moods, the way you think, your blind spots, and your passions. Let them guide you.

3. **Have a really big, big picture.**

When you know your long-term goals, have a vision, or have a helicopter view of the current situation or opportunity, you'll have more information on which to base your decisions.

4. **Always have a Plan B, Plan C, and Plan D ready to go!**

You can improve your good judgment by having backup plans, whether you need them or not.

5. **Don't put yourself in situations where you are forced to rely too much on your "good judgment."**

This one is important. Consistent good decisions help you avoid situations where having "good judgment" becomes critical. Don't confuse good judgment with good crisis management.

6. **Separate the facts from the interpretation of the facts.**

There are very few facts that aren't also coupled with someone's interpretation of the facts. Either sales are down 20 percent or they are not. An explanation is just that. There are great explanations, few of which are worth banking your business on. If sales are down, assume they'll stay down until you do something about it.

7. **Always include a worst-case scenario—and make it a really bad scenario.**

For a decade or two, Detroit kept factoring in worst-case scenarios, yet they continually came up short. They took incremental actions based on what they wanted to believe would happen, and not what was so clearly a long-term trend of foreign-made cars slicing up their market share. Living in denial is always expensive—yet we all do it. A good way to get out of denial is to assume that sales will drop 50 percent in the next year and be ready for that possibility. Just by including that possibility and developing options at that level, you'll make better decisions about what is more likely to happen.

8. Always look at the downside of every decision you make.

If you're adding a new product, increasing the customer service budget, reducing overhead, permitting use of your trademark, or entering into a co-venture agreement, make a list of the ten potentially negative and even deadly consequences of even a highly positive change. Everything affects everything today— and unexpectedly. If you respect this ecological truth you'll realize that every decision affects you, your employees, your shareholders, your profitability, and your viability.

9. Seek to enhance your reputation first and your bottom line second.

I used to base most of my decisions on whether or not my company would make more money. But then I realized that the future of my business came from my current customers, their word-of-mouth, and from the press we were beginning to receive from the national media. At that point, it occurred to me that if I'd just invest more money in our reputation and make my decisions based more on reputation than quarterly profitability, I'd be a lot more financially successful—and more proud of my company, too.

10. Surround yourself with others who have excellent judgment.

There are so many subtleties about acquiring and developing good judgment that most of the process comes best from friends, colleagues, competitors, and staff who already have great judgment. Learn from them, in every conversation.

Ways to Bring Out the Best in Others

1. Expect more of them than you do of yourself.

2. Challenge *them* to discover what brings out their best.

3. Help people to discover their values so that what they do professionally is an expression of those values.

4. Ask: "What is it that you do not now have in your life that you want in your life?"

5. Ask: "What is it that you are not now doing that you want to be doing?"

6. Ask: "What is it that you are now doing that you want to *stop* doing?"

7. Ask: "What is it that you are doing that's okay, but that you want to do better?"

8. Identify and remove the perceived consequences of failure or making mistakes; this
often frees up a person's natural "best."

9. Bring the person back to age six or twelve and
help them get in touch with what they wanted
for themselves at that time—this can shed
some light on a person's "lost" aspirations.

10. Spend thirty minutes with someone, asking
questions, hearing their responses, and asking
more questions as you get deeper into
uncovering their goals.

THE TOP 10 TEN
Things to Do When Accountability Is Missing

1. Inform the employee that he is not being accountable and find out why.

2. Ask the employee how he plans to solve that problem and press him for a real solution rather than just promises.

3. Install consequences so that both parties know exactly what will happen if the solution is not implemented.

4. Help the employee become accountable by installing hourly or daily reporting, even if it sounds remedial.

5. Find out why the employee's integrity is low—that's usually the source of waning accountability.

6. Find a better position for the employee. He may just be bored or have outgrown his job.

7. Train the employee in the skills of account-ability. *Teach* him how to be accountable, don't assume he already knows.

8. Identify and remove whatever is in the way of him being accountable. It could be missing tools or a poor structure.

9. Impress upon the employee that accountability is a joy, not a "should."

10. Make the employee accountable for someone else as well!

Keys to Effective, Flexible Management

1. Give the person a huge goal that will keep her attention. Ask her to develop the strategies or steps to achieve the goal.

2. Have daily or weekly reports or check-ins (daily at first).

3. Ask the person how willing she is to be effectively managed. Also inform her of your particular style and of your high standards.

4. Get the person focused on actions and outcomes, not just goal setting and reporting.

5. Install a system that warns you *before* the person stops performing.

6. Build in coaching to your conversations so that the person understands that you aren't just managing her to reach goals, but that you are helping her to become a more effective person.

7. Build your staff so that you can afford for them not to produce. You should be able to fire them if necessary, as this will free you up to manage well rather than be fearful or reactive.

8. Rather than expecting your staff to know everything, seek to provide answers, tools, and support *before* they need it.

9. Don't get too chummy with your staff. Be a manager who has a lot going on and make sure the staff knows that you're relying on them to do their best without coddling.

10. Develop a visual display of results, progress, and problems and post this for everyone to see. This keeps the facts public and is very motivational.

Secrets for Retaining Key Employees

1. Give them an economic stake, notably equity or options. Everyone's an entrepreneur these days, especially key employees!

2. Offer key employees a way to get around *anything* or *anyone* that gets in the way of their creativity, effectiveness, or productivity.

3. Develop a company mission that is even more compelling than any one individual is. This bonds key employees.

4. Create an entrepreneurial environment which stimulates without becoming adversarial or territorial.

5. Give key employees the *best* of every tool, software, or equipment. They appreciate these more than the average employee.

6. Challenge key employees to produce *far more* than they currently are producing. Key employees need challenges to keep them focused and out of mischief—or job searching!

7. Eliminate the traditional power structure and replace it with a strength-based power structure in order to reduce politics and simplify management levels.

8. Offer key employees continuous training, both in their skill set and in management skills training programs.

9. Build up the reputations of key employees. Don't be afraid to grant them this visibility and credibility.

10. Put key employees in their own 'club' so they *know* they are one of the anointed ones. They'll be motivated by it.

Techniques for Effective Delegating

1. Delegate outcomes, don't dump problems.

Recognize the difference.

2. Only delegate to people that you trust. Period.

Don't delegate and hope for the best.

3. Point out the consequences to the company and yourself if what you're delegating isn't successfully managed.

Sure, you can also include the consequences to the delegatee, but it usually works best for them to get a picture of what's at stake.

4. Delegate small pieces at first, then more.

Make sure that they've handled the small pieces perfectly before you give them more.

5. Install a reporting system, so that you can catch little problems way before they become overwhelming.

It's not a matter of trusting or not trusting the delegatee; it's a matter of your well-being and absence of fear. Facts reassure.

6. **Ask the delegatee to develop the milestones, midpoints, phases, even if you know what they should be.**

Let the delegatee create this as it will increase his or her ownership in the project.

7. **Don't delegate what should be automated.**

Before you delegate anything, find out how to eliminate the step altogether.

8. **Don't delegate what only you can do accurately.**

This is controversial, but I suggest that you become so fast at the critical tasks that you actually do stuff which traditionally "could" or "should" be delegated.

9. **If you can't find good people to delegate to, learn from *that.***

It may mean that you're not built to delegate or that you're a creative type (Would Picasso have delegated? Doubtful.), or that you just haven't attracted the right people yet in your business or life. If that's the case, just keep doing stuff yourself—you're probably just not ready to delegate.

10. **Spend three times more time with the delegatee than you think you should.**

They really do need you. Spend your time being in touch, massaging them or the process, listening for errors in judgment, removing obstacles, and so on. Don't delegate-it-and-forget-it! It's not fair to your project or your delegatee.

TOP 10 TEN

Ways to Condition Others to Change

1. Educate everyone in advance on the rate of change in their job, the company, your life, and so on, so that they won't be surprised.

2. Let people know about the change you are planning before you actually need them to change.

3. Establish an agreement with people so that they will be willing to change rather than be rigid.

4. Be up front and fully honest.

   Change is scary enough, but when the other person feels like they don't have all of the information, resistance will be more intense.

5. As soon as you or the situation changes in some way, let others know immediately.

   Don't wait for the right time or place to disclose news. Waiting only makes it harder for everyone.

6. Put the change into perspective.

   Be clear why things must change—link the change to world events, business trends, other themes so that folks realize that they are part of something much larger than the change that you are presenting to them.

7. **Be up front about the consequences, if any, if they don't adopt the change.**

People need to know what their options are.

8. **Be patient while people reposition themselves after first learning about the change.**

The body and mind take time to make this adjustment, so don't assume a sluggish response is resistance—it's just human nature.

9. **Have a Change Day once a month to announce all of the changes in a thoughtful way.**

This will let folks get used to lots of change and perhaps even look forward to it.

10. **Demonstrate the change.**

It's important that folks can see that you've embraced the change instead of just asking them to change. Be a model that they can emulate.

Keys to Helping Employees Participate More Actively

1. Design work around the individuals' strengths. Don't just slot people into jobs.

2. Have lots of contact with each person, either individually or in a group setting. Presence equals participation.

3. Set a target, vision, or goal that is naturally motivating or compelling—the "gap" creates a vacuum.

4. Put everyone on e-mail, the Internet, conference calls, Lotus Notes, and so on, so that each person contributes to the group's agenda not just you as the leader.

5. Identify the mavericks and help them develop work around existing bureaucracy and limitations.

6. Keep people so busy that they don't have time to slack off.

7. Budget time to listen to the troublemakers, complainers, and envelope-pushers—they often have the wisdom you need even if the packaging is torn.

8. Change meetings from boring reporting sessions into creative sessions. Reporting should be automated.

9. If you're not a good motivator, find someone on the team who is and delegate this function to them.

10. Remove the employees who just don't get it, are too negative, aren't helpful—don't spend too much time trying to fix or convert them.

Ways to Eliminate the Politics In Your Company

1. Accept that politics are inherent and natural.

In any power-based structure (companies, government, institutions, etc.), politics are present.

2. Seek to understand the dynamic of politics.

Politics within a company can be healthful and indicative. Don't assume that you should try to eradicate it.

3. Build up the firm's culture until the culture permeates the company and becomes larger than politics.

A strong, cooperative company culture outclasses politics; it's the perfect antidote.

4. Set goals that are so large that people don't have time for politics.

The objectives and needs of the firm will displace politics, out of necessity.

5. Fire the politicians.

No matter what you do, some people are just power players to the point of being destructive. If they won't change their ways, get rid of them, even if they are effective. The cost is too great— you'll lose other employees unless you eliminate the source of the cancer.

6. **Keep your reporting systems so clean that politics and gossip have no place to fester.**

When the integrity is strong and when everyone already knows what others are doing in their jobs, gossip drops significantly.

7. **Be up front and over communicate everything about the company that may in any way affect any employee.**

Don't put positive spins on bad news and don't withhold key information. With trust, the power of politics diminishes.

8. **Inform employees how to get ahead in the company.**

Give everyone an equal shot. They'll know it if you're playing favorites.

9. **Teach employees to solve their own problems, especially conflicts with other employees.**

This is far more than sensitivity training or communication basics—teach your staff the benefits of communication. Then they'll do it because they want to.

10. **Teach your staff how to get along with coworkers with opposing styles.**

Again, this is far more than diversity training—it's valuable information that will result in less background noise getting in the way of people working cooperatively. With cooperation, the effects of politics are minimized.

THE TOP 10 TEN

Ways to Turn a Complainer into a Positive Person

1. Most complainers are oblivious to the fact that they whine or complain as much as they do.

By not pointing it out, you're tolerating it.

2. Insist that people change their complaint into a clear request.

This is incredibly easy to do! Just remind them to do it, the moment you hear them going down that path.

3. Ask them to become a completely positive person when with you.

They'll look at you funny, but it's better than putting up with complaints.

4. Find out what is really bothering them.

A complaint is usually a symptom.

5. Hear every complaint from clients and potential customers as a way to make more money.

This is more than a mind set—it's really an effective way to increase profits if you'll just hear the complaints as a consumer wanting to buy more or buy more easily.

6. Stop complaining yourself.

When you stop, others stop.

7. Let people know that you don't do well with complaints.

"Bob, I'm so bad at hearing complaints. Let's focus on something that you're excited about, OK?"

8. Surround yourself only with naturally positive people.

Sometimes, it's just not worth trying to change people.

9. Focus the other person on an outcome that they really want.

Try saying something like, "If you could have it exactly as you want it, tell me what that would look like."

10. Look surprised when they start complaining.

Say something like: "Why, George, I never knew you to be a complainer! This must really be bad!"

THE TOP 10 TEN

Ways to Keep Your Finger on the Pulse

1. Design the measures of success and failure in your business.

2. Get daily and weekly reports that tell you worthwhile measurables.

3. Spend one day a week with your best customers—listening, collaborating, suggesting, understanding.

4. Spend half a day each week answering phones—from customers, prospective customers, the public.

5. Have a monthly meeting with your competitors, discussing the trends of your field and ways to cooperate.

6. Have about a dozen "agents" in every aspect of your business who will tell you the truth.

7. Watch how your customers actually *use* (and misuse) your product or service.

8. Stay ahead of your business by reading magazines that keep you informed about worldwide technological and lifestyle trends.

9. Avoid delegating key, even if minor, tasks that matter most to your customers.

10. Instill the above nine items in the minds and hearts of your employees (and customers!) so that you don't have to rely on your ear only.

7

BUSINESS
WISDOM

Undervalued Strengths of Most Companies

Good companies have a lot of strengths. Some strengths, though, aren't very "sexy," and so don't get the credit they deserve. But be careful; neglect your company's hidden strengths and they could soon slip away.

1. Low, low cost-structure and overhead.

Required today to stay competitive.

2. Internet-centricity.

Management team that is Web-savvy and Web-oriented.

3. Integrity/reserve levels.

High level of employee's time/space/production reserve (extra). With reserve comes improved judgment, fewer errors, space to see/create the future, time to do complete work and ability to maintain integrity.

4. Star salespeople.

Managed and invested in properly, the star salesperson can double again their performance, even if it means they are producing 3–10 times the average of others.

5. Vision.

Size, scope and outrageousness of the company's mission or vision attracts talented people and raises standards more than traditional motivation.

6. Trust and super-conductivity.

Level of trust naturally occurring within the organization permits a free flow of information and permits problems to be solved immediately.

7. Innovation-ability.

It's about quantity, quality, and the rate at which new stuff is being created or the value being added to current products and services.

8. Proximity to customers.

The closer the company is to the consumers/beneficiaries of their products/services, the better products they will produce, sooner, maintaining their advantage.

9. Ability to adapt, quickly.

The rate that the company's systems reengineer and adapt, automatically, can be increased.

10. The reward system.

There are very creative ways to motivate and reward for performance, risk-taking, innovation, leadership, initiative, creativity, efficiency, and effectiveness.

Predictions for Boards of Directors

1. Boards will be smaller as the need grows for fewer, more decisive board members who can act upon issues with "warp-speed" immediacy.

2. Wisdom and experience will be at a premium, so mandatory term limits for board members (now common) will be "an idea whose time has passed," as Augustine says.

3. There will be more retirees (now in disfavor) on boards as the trend of executives retiring earlier continues and as people live longer, more productive lives.

4. While they won't have to be rocket scientists, directors will be more competent in understanding technology and its implications than is the case today.

5. Boards will be meeting less often face-to-face and more often in cyberspace.

6. As boards meet less frequently, board committees will do more work and become more powerful.

7. There will be a complete passing from the scene of the director who sits on ten or more boards.

8. Directors will have to serve as an "on call" consultant to the company, working not only with the CEO but, depending on the director's expertise, with other managers.

9. When companies get into trouble, twenty-first-century social and regulatory pressures will cause Japan-style resignations by disgraced board members.

10. Finally, executives now coming of age to be directors in the next century have spent the formative years of their careers in an era of uncertainty and change, which will make them more aggressive directors compared with the generation of board members they will be replacing which grew up in a "go-go" era for business.

THE TOP 10 TEN

Moments of Truth for a Business

1. Logo

2. Phone number

3. Advertising

4. Customer service center

5. Product or service

6. Packaging

7. Pricing

8. Performance

9. Reputation

10. Warranty/refunds

Business Maxims

1. Never stop learning.

2. Never accept that there isn't a better way to do things.

3. Practice management by wandering around— stay close to your people.

4. Show every person respect. Encourage the sharing of ideas.

5. Practice excellence in everything you do.

6. Never compromise your integrity. Deliver on your promises.

7. Feel good about yourself.

8. Learn that you don't have to win every issue. Compromise is often necessary in every area except for point number six above.

9. Learn to balance your life between work, home, and social responsibilities.

10. Listen very carefully.

Ways to Become a Known Expert

1. Invent something new: a product, service, idea, solution.

When you're first, who can prove you wrong? And there's no competition!

2. Get quoted by the media.

Once you get quoted a couple of times, you're set.

3. Get a book published.

Instant credibility. Even if you don't make any money on the book, you'll find it's a magnet for new business and far better than a business card.

4. Pull off at least one miracle with a client in a difficult situation.

Results, especially in tricky and impossible situations, speak for themselves. If you've turned a bad company around or helped a client lose 100 pounds or turned Madonna into a virgin—word will get around and you'll have a chance to prove your abilities again.

5. Get featured by the media.

It is not difficult to get covered by the media if you're doing anything that's interesting. And, one feature story leads to another.

6. Give talks, even locally.

Breakfast clubs, Rotary meetings, associations, luncheons. You'll find that you'll naturally attract bigger and more prestigious venues, leading to keynotes.

7. Have fans and followers.

If others (clients or colleagues) view you as an expert in something, their feelings are contagious and soon others will start seeing you the same way.

8. Get other important/credentialed people to endorse you.

You can become highly regarded just by the company you keep. Don't be afraid to approach the well-known and ask for their support! If you're good, it's to their advantage to endorse you.

9. Develop a track record that proves how good you are.

Go create a couple of successes with your ideas, skills, business, service, etc., and you're off to a good start. People want to see evidence before they'll treat you with the respect you deserve.

10. Set up a structure to add to your stature.

Set up a think tank, an association, a training firm, a publishing company, a content-rich Web site—anything to give others yet another way to hear about you.

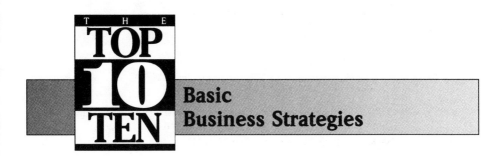

THE TOP 10 TEN
Basic Business Strategies

1. Become #1.

2. Stay #1.

3. Create a new niche or fill a niche need.

4. Expand your product line.

5. Push your brand name and leverage it.

6. Increase high-profit sales only.

7. Increase revenue substantially.

8. Increase return-on-equity.

9. Cut expenses significantly.

10. Turn the company around.

ACKNOWLEDGMENTS

We are grateful to the many people who contributed top-ten lists to our Web site, in particular the following, whose lists we used in this book:

Shale Paul
Marty Crouch
Dominick Bencivenga
James Vuocolo
Margaret Krigbaum
Hans Kohler

Thank you for allowing us to include your wisdom.

We also extend our thanks to Ray Bard and Scott Bard for fostering the creation of the book, Sara Schroeder for her manuscript development efforts, and Steve Welch for copyediting that tightened the impact of the lists. Suzanne Pustejovsky's inviting text design and Hugh Pirnie's bold cover design captured the essence of the book. Thanks also to Sherry Sprague for her project management and Deborah Costenbader and Doreen Piano for proofreading. Without the efforts of these people, you would not have the book you hold in your hand today.

On behalf of the contributors, editors, and designers, we hope this book brings you "working wisdom."

ABOUT COACH UNIVERSITY

Coach University was founded by Thomas Leonard in 1992 to train personal and business coaches. The program consists of thirty-six core training modules, each of which is a four-hour TeleClass delivered one hour per week, over the phone, by a trained leader. The classes, which average eighteen students, combine instruction, role play, and discussion.

To learn more about becoming a coach, call 800-48-COACH and request our forty-eight-page Coach Information Kit. You can also take a four-hour TeleClass called "123 Coach," a free introduction to coaching that will teach you some of the basic skills we cover in the program.

For a more comprehensive look at what Coach University has to offer, visit our web site at www.coachu.com.

For additional copies

of

WORKING WISDOM

Top 10 Lists for Improving Your Business

Visit your favorite bookstore

or

Call Toll-free

1-800-945-3132

or

Fax 512-288-5055

24 hours a day

Seven days a week

VISA/MasterCard/American Express/Discover accepted

Quantity discounts are available